P9-CAJ-891

TABLE OF CONTENTS

Fact. More than 50 million people in the United States bowl during a year. Fact. Nearly four million compete regularly in league play sanctioned by the American Bowling Congress, Women's International Bowling Congress and Young American Bowling Alliance.

Bowling has soared into the upper echelon of sports, setting a steady pace by blending strong organization with modern centers in which to participate. Although the sport now appeals to people from all walks of life, entering a bowling center today would give few clues to its origin.

Bowling has been traced to articles found in the tomb of an Egyptian child buried in 5200 B.C.

The primitive implements included nine pieces of stone at which a stone "ball" was rolled, the ball having first to roll through an archway made of three pieces of marble.

Another ancient discovery was the Polynesian game of ula maika, also utilizing pins and balls of stone.

The stones were to be rolled at targets 60 feet away, a distance

history of bowling

"On entering the amphitheater, new objects of wonder presented themselves. On a level spot in the centre was a company of odd-looking personages playing at ninepins... Nothing interrupted the stillness of the scene but the noise of the balls, which, whenever they were rolled, echoed along the mountains like rumbling peals of thunder..."

from Rip Van Winkle
-Washington Irving

which today still is one of the basic regulations of tenpins.

Bowling at pins probably originated in ancient Germany, not as a sport but as a religious ceremony. Martin Luther is credited with settling on nine as the ideal number of pins.

The game moved throughout Europe, the Scandinavian countries, and finally to the United States, with the earliest known reference to bowling at pins in America made by author Washington Irving about 1818 in "Rip Van Winkle."

The game was being played throughout the world and rules were different almost everywhere. Even basic equipment was not the same. In fact, why and when the extra pin was added from the European game of ninepins to the American game of tenpins remains a mystery.

Regardless of how the game came into being, it became so popular by mid-19th century

indoor lanes were being built throughout Manhattan and the Bronx and on westward, in Syracuse, Buffalo, Cincinnati, Chicago, Milwaukee and other cities with large German populations.

In 1875, delegates from nine bowling clubs in New York and Brooklyn met in Germania Hall in the Bowery and organized the National Bowling Association. This was the first attempt to bring order out of chaos.

Disagreement raged between East and West, principally the alignment of New York State bowlers against everyone else to the west. On Sept. 9, 1895, the American Bowling Congress was organized in Beethoven Hall in New York City (see page 6).

A group of 40 women, encouraged by proprietor Dennis J. Sweeney of St. Louis, met at Sweeney's establishment in 1916 and formed what today is known as the Women's International Bowling Congress (see page 10).

Basic concepts of the American Bowling Congress have remained unchanged since its founding in 1895. Staff at ABC headquarters in suburban Milwaukee works closely with approximately 2,800 local associations to serve more than two million members.

ABC's roots can be traced to many people. One was Thomas Curtis, who became ABC's first president and chaired several historic meetings which produced an organization which succeeded where others had failed.

The adoption of rules at the Sept. 9, 1895 meeting in Beethoven Hall, and most important, the distribution of nearly 1,000 copies by mail to bowling groups in many parts of the United States, was the move which created interest and trust in the fledgling group. Within a few

210 BEETHOVEN HALL

months, there were members in Buffalo; New York; Cincinnati; Lowell, Mass.; Boston; Chicago; St. Louis; Wheeling, W.Va.; Kansas City, and Quebec.

Ever since, representatives of local, state and provincial associations like these have annually met in convention to review rules and consider proposed changes. Also elected are officers and directors, all of whom serve voluntarily and without pay. The only exceptions are the executive director and assistant director, who oversee the home office staff.

Service has been ABC's aim since its early days. Service begins when a league is formed and applies for sanction. The sanction, with membership cards distributed to each bowler, gives ABC a record of its membership and entitles the league and its members to the following services:

• Automatic bonding to protect bowler funds from theft, burglary and misuse.

• Awards for every level of achievement from 300 games to 700 and 800 series to league champions, most improved league bowlers and those who bowl a game of 100 and a series of 150 or more pins above or more pins above average.

• Essential tools for league officers including rulebooks, schedules, handicap charts, average calculators and other aids.

• Rules advice and counseling.

• Free tournament sanctioning.

• Equally important in maintaining standard bowling conditions are the programs of lane certification and equipment testing and research. Every lane is checked and measured each season to assure it meets ABC/Women's International Bowling Congress specifications. Pins, automatic pinsetting machines, scoring devices and other allied equipment undergo thorough and lengthy testing before receiving approval for use in ABC sanctioned league or tournament competition.

the history

In their own ways, baseball great Babe Ruth (left) and Jeremy Sonnenfeld, the first person to roll an approved 900 series, are legends in bowling.

• Publicizing the inner workings of the Congress, as well as the feats of bowlers coast to coast, is the role of the Public Relations department. Bowlers are as well informed as any sports group in the world through ABC's publication, *Bowling Magazine,* and through news releases, pamphlets, brochures and other publications.

Although the service programs have been thorough, new groups created special attention. In 1963, ABC added a Seniors program and designed a complete set of services for the nation's senior citizens. The ABC National Seniors Tournament for men 55 and older was initiated in 1964 and expanded to reach every state in 1982.

In 1966, a Collegiate Division was initiated by the Congress to provide a program for the nation's college men while at the same time bridging the service gap between junior and adult competition.

With the formation of the Young American Bowling Alliance in 1982, the Collegiate Division became a part of that organization. It was returned to the ABC/WIBC in 1998 and renamed College Bowling USA.

The most spectacular of ABC's many services is the national championship tournament, the oldest bowling event in the nation. A fixture on the sports scene since 1901, it is unrivaled as a participant spectacle. Held in America's major cities, the ABC Tournament runs 12 to 16 hours daily for more than 100 consecutive days.

On lanes specially-installed in public arenas, as many as 17,000 teams and 92,000 individuals participate each year. The prize fund approaches $3 million.

The glamour event of the ABC Tournament is the Masters, which matches the world's greatest bowlers in head-to-head double elimination competition following qualifying round play. Each match consists of three games throughout the competition unless the finals are televised. In that event, a stepladder format takes precedent.

ABC started a new tournament in 1992 aimed at bringing the sport back to its team roots. The Brunswick/ABC World Team Challenge features a nationwide qualifying tour leading to a Grand Championships where U.S. teams are joined by foreign squads.

In conjunction with WIBC, ABC launched the Festival of Bowling in 1999. It provides a wide variety of formats for bowlers to enter as often as they like.

Whether through leagues or tournaments, ABC provides its members with options, all with the aim of having fun.

For more information about ABC, visit **www.bowl.com**.

Former U.S. President Harry Truman was among the first chief executives to discover bowling.

There are many colorful stories about when women began bowling in the United States. Seniors reminisce about the turn of the century, when their mothers or grandmothers sneaked in with (or without) their husbands to try out the bowling game. Often they did so at the risk of their reputations.

Tales are told about women bowlers being screened off from view behind partitions or drapes or being allowed to bowl only when men were not using the alleys. Those were the days of high button shoes, skirts to the ankles, cumbersome apparel and tenpin accommodations that were hardly appealing.

Old photos document scenes of women bowling as early as the 1880s. The first recorded formalized bowling for women began in 1907 in St. Louis, when Dennis J. Sweeney, a bowling proprietor and sports writer, organized a women's league.

Bowling proprietor and sports writer Dennis Sweeney of St. Louis helped found WIBC in 1916.

Inklings of national interest also were being shown. That same year (1907) many women accompanied their husbands to the American Bowling Congress Tournament in St. Louis, as they had been doing for several years. In St. Louis the women laid plans to hold their own tournament the following year, on ABC Tournament lanes in Cincinnati after the annual men's event had concluded. A second women's tournament in 1909 followed the ABC event in Pittsburgh.

Records show little activity until 1915, when Ellen Kelly, an avid bowler, formed the St. Louis Women's Bowling Association. Buoyed by her success, she wrote to proprietors across the country asking for names of women who might be interested in a national organization of their own. She followed with letters to those women, urging the organization of local associations and offering advice on rules and establishing an organization.

By the Fall of 1916 in St. Louis, Sweeney was there to help Mrs. Kelly stage the first "national tournament." There were eight teams entered and champions were decided in team, doubles, singles and all events. The prize fund was $225.

Following the tournament those 40 women from 11 cities met at Sweeney's Washington Recreation Parlor and created the national organization that became after several name changes – the Women's International Bowling Congress. Fifty years later a charter member described the initial tournament as "frankly plain, there were eight alleys and four rows of benches for visitors, a small counter square in back of the benches was used to sell soda pop, popcorn, peanuts, etc." She also recalled that the "meeting was more of a social gathering, and we gave little thought that it would develop into such a big organization."

The 40 pioneers elected their first national officers and adopted a constitution and bylaws that included the following purposes: To provide, adopt and enforce uniform rules and regulations governing the play of American tenpins; to provide and enforce uniform qualifications for tournaments and their participants; to hold a national tournament, and to encourage good feeling and create interest in the bowling game.

Those original precepts became the foundation of WIBC, which has developed into the largest sports organization in the world for women. The 40 pioneers set the pattern for today's 1.5 million WIBC members, who bowl in more than 80,000 sanctioned leagues in approximately 2,700 local associations in every state and several foreign countries.

That humble national tournament – with its eight team entry – was the forerunner of what is now the largest women's sports event in the world. In fact, the 1997 WIBC Championship tournament held in Reno, Nev., attracted 14,872 five woman teams, the largest entry for any team tournament in history. There were 88,279 individuals, a women's world record.

That first tentative gathering on the benches in Washington Recreation Parlor has evolved into a model of bowling democracy, the WIBC Annual Meeting. More than 3,000 delegates representing local and state associations attend the WIBC Annual Meeting to adopt rules and select national leaders. Similar annual meetings at local, state and provincial levels assure

the self-government concept. Nationally, WIBC is governed by a board of directors elected by the delegates. Administrative policies and procedures are implemented by a staff at WIBC headquarters in suburban Milwaukee.

Along with growth and development have come a multiplicity of services. Leagues receive a wealth of rule books, record keeping materials and prepackaged kits to keep them functioning smoothly. Local, state and provincial associations benefit from a variety of materials to help them conduct their affairs more efficiently, ranging from handbooks, information

sheets and forms to educational seminars, workshops and counseling from staff members and field representatives. A bonding and insurance program provided by WIBC covers association and league funds. A tournament sanctioning program is another important service.

A description of WIBC's awards for members would fill a chapter in itself. They recognize achievements within the realm of every bowler, from the beginner to the world champion.

Since its humble beginnings, WIBC has stood for tradition, friendship, fun, competition, leadership and success.

Since 1916, it has meant this and more to the millions of women who have proudly called WIBC "my organization."

Those words retain their special meaning today.

For more information about WIBC, visit the **www.bowl.com** web site.

Aug. 1, 1982 was an historic day, one that found the Young American Bowling Alliance officially joining the bowling family.

YABA is the result of combining three groups – American Junior Bowling Congress, Youth Bowling Association and ABC/WIBC Collegiate Division – into one.

Organized bowling for young people began in 1936 in Chicago when Milt Raymer, a high school teacher, organized an intramural league. Its success led to a city-wide program with more than 8,000 boys and girls taking part. The National Bowling Council provided financial support in 1945 to expand the program nationally and the following year it became the AJBC.

In 1962 Charles F. Hall was appointed head of AJBC and his

leadership resulted in continued growth. Hall became YABA's first executive director in 1982.

The YBA was formed for the 1963-64 season by the Bowling Proprietors Association of America, and during that time AJBC was co-sponsored by ABC and WIBC. Membership continued to grow in both groups.

The ABC initiated the Collegiate Division in 1966 to provide a program for the nation's college men. The Association of College Unions International began a championships competition conducted annually on the ABC Tournament lanes. The ABC/WIBC Collegiate Division was created in the mid-1970s and a similar ACUI event for women has been staged at the WIBC tournament ever since.

The Collegiate Division was turned over to YABA when it was formed, then back to ABC/WIBC under the name College Bowling USA in 1998.

YABA encourages healthy competition, physical fitness, sportsmanship and good citizenship. It is designed to provide all youth the opportunity to learn the skills of bowling and to participate in organized play. Providing playing rules and supervision, along with leadership and teaching programs, YABA is dedicated to giving everyone the opportunity to bowl and maintain amateur status.

YABA provides the following membership services:

•Program material for organizing leagues, including schedules, handicap tables, award

applications, membership cards, record forms and secretary's handbook.

• Extensive awards program featuring emblems, plaques, medals and certificates for individual and team accomplishments. Awards are determined by age classification for Bantam, Prep, Junior, Major and Senior members.

• Special individual awards are available for all-spare games, triplicates, 100 pins over average, 7-10 and 4-6-7-10 split conversions and Dutch 200.

• Honor scores of 298, 299 and 300 games and 800 series for boys and girls plus 700 series for girls earn special awards.

• National awards are provided to the top 10 scorers in each age division for the season and are publicized on the YABA portion of the industry web site – **www.bowl.com**.

Adult leadership and guidance are of great importance to young bowlers.

More than 15,000 coaches and league officials provide fundamental and advanced instruction, and guidance and example in etiquette and sportsmanship.

Coaching schools provide training for adults and league assistants and teach juniors to become student coaches.

The Youth Leader program helps young people learn to assume a wide range of responsibility, serving on association committees, planning and conducting tournaments and assisting in instructing handicapped bowlers.

Tournament sanctioning and guidelines for tournaments are provided associations and state/provincial YABA groups. In the Coca-Cola Junior Bowling Championships, entrants earn scholarships at the local, state and national level. At the USA Junior Olympic Gold National Championships, youth compete for spots on USA Junior Olympic Bowling/TEAM USA.™

YABA also has put together an Athlete Development Pipeline. This is designed to guide both serious and recreational youth bowlers through the different stages of development in the sport, teaching them how to improve and compete on all levels.

YABA helps members build confidence, develop athletic ability, enhance social skills, learn leadership skills, start life-long friendships and learn teamwork. But most important, they have fun.

And while they're having fun, they learn that bowling can help them pay for college or technical school. YABA leagues and tournaments raise more than $3 million annually in scholarship money.

Youth bowlers know bowling rocks, it's cool and it's a blast. YABA makes it easier to grab their friends, the kids from school or family members and check out all the excitement.

YABA MISSION STATEMENT

The Young American Bowling Alliance is the premier international youth membership organization in the sport of tenpin bowling. We are committed to providing fun, excitement and opportunities for the personal development of youth.

USA BOWLING

USA Bowling is among the newer organizations in bowling, but its responsibilities are world-wide. One of the organization's main duties is to select United States representatives for international competition.

Founded as the United States Tenpin Bowling Federation in the summer of 1989 by the ABC and WIBC, it became USA Bowling in 1993.

Governed by a 12-member board which includes three athletes, USA Bowling is recognized by the U.S. Olympic Committee and the Federation Internationale des Quilleurs as the governing body for the sport in the U.S.

It coordinates all amateur international competition promoted by USOC or FIQ, and conducts the USA Bowling Championships. In addition, it is the leader in providing instruction and coaching programs to help bowlers advance in ability.

USA Bowling's Coaching Certification Program has trained more than 2,800 people as it strives toward the goal of having certified coaches available to all bowlers across the country. The program features three levels – Bronze, Silver and Gold. It remains the only bowling coaching program approved by the U.S. Olympic Committee.

The U.S. has been represented in international competition since the 1930s when the late Dr. Joe Thum, a New York City proprietor later elected to the ABC Hall of Fame, organized teams to travel to Europe. Prior to the 1936 Olympics in Berlin, Germany, a large delegation of male bowlers participated in a special event. Bowling was an exhibition sport at the 1988 Olympics in Seoul South Korea, and has been part of four Pan American Games.

For more information about USA Bowling, visit **www.bowl.com**.

USA BOWLING MISSION STATEMENT

USA Bowling's mission is to continue as the world leader in bowling while consistently winning gold medals in international competition, advance the skill level of all bowlers and coaches and to achieve Olympic medal status.

BPAA MISSION STATEMENT

It is the mission of BPAA to enhance the profitability of its members

FEDERATION INTERNATIONALE DES QUILLEURS

The Federation Internationale des Quilleurs is the world governing body of bowling with 110 member federations in 88 countries located in all five Olympic zones.

The FIQ was founded in 1952 with nine nations. It first applied for International Olympic Committee recognition in 1963, and finally was officially recognized in 1979. It was an official exhibition sport in the 1988 Games.

FIQ regulates two disciplines: tenpin and ninepin. Ninepin is concentrated primarily on the European continent. Tenpin, played worldwide, has three geographical zones (American, Asian and European). Both disciplines conduct many world and regional championships for men, women and youth. FIQ is included in the following international and regional championships: Pan American Games; Asian Games; World Games; Commonweath Games; Central and South American Games; Caribbean Games; Bolvarian Games; South East and Far East Asian Games; Maccabiah Games; Masters Games; Solidarity Games, and Ciss Games.

The U.S. became an FIQ member in 1961, making its official international debut in the 1963 FIQ World Championships in Mexico.

BOWLING PROPRIETORS ASSOCIATION OF AMERICA

The Bowling Proprietors Association of America, organized in 1932, is a coalition of proprietors, with common goals and challenges, working together at the local, state and national levels.

The BPAA relies on the state associations to help implement its programs and services and to help communicate membership benefits to local proprietors. It also conducts a widely popular annual international trade show convention.

In conjunction with the other major bowling organizations, BPAA is working to strengthen bowling's standing worldwide.

During the 1997-98 season, the bowling industry came to realize that college bowling is a major link in the progression of people who bowl and that youth and college demographics are the largest growing and influential group in the current and future entertainment business. Thus, the Intercollegiate Bowling Program came out with a new look and name, College Bowling USA.

both recreational and intercollegiate bowling on college campuses.

It is believed the first collegiate bowling competition was held at Yale University on April 8, 1916, nearly eight months before the Women's International Bowling Congress was formed. After the competition, leaders of the six Eastern schools entered formed the Intercollegiate Bowling Association.

ABC and the WIBC adopted legislation to administer College Bowling USA and its championship tournaments, effective the 1998-99 season. Today, College Bowling USA works with and promotes

Little is written about college bowling between then and the 1940s when many events were held in the East and Midwest. This led to the development of the American Bowling Congress and WIBC having their own college programs during the

1966-67 season. As the program grew, ABC and WIBC decided to combine their programs and efforts to become the ABC and WIBC Collegiate Division during the 1977-78 season.

In 1982, the Young American Bowling Alliance was formed and the industry decided collegiate bowling belonged to the youth division. Thus, during the 1982-83 season the program became the YABA Collegiate Division.

For various reasons, over the next several years college bowling began to deteriorate.

To revitalize it, YABA implemented the Campus Program. This focused on the recreational verses the intercollegiate side of bowling to help create a greater awareness of bowling on college campuses from which more intercollegiate programs would result.

This theory proved true as intercollegiate membership peaked during the 1990-91 season with 209 colleges featuring more than 3,000 individuals. During the 1991-92 season campus programs peaked on their own with 71 colleges having programs and more than 26,000 individual members.

Due to lack of resources, however, the campus program was phased out during the 1994-95 season and the overall management of the college bowling was put under general YABA tournament and events. YABA then started looking at where college bowling really belonged since most members were ABC and WIBC not YABA.

In 1994 a major boost occurred for college bowling when the National Collegiate Athletic Association recognized women's bowling as an emerging sport to help settle federal gender equity issues in college sports. With this development the bowling industry did not want college bowling to end so it formed an industry joint oversight committee that operated college bowling using joint funding from ABC, WIBC and YABA. Thus, during the 1995-96 season the Intercollegiate Bowling Program was formed, later expanding to include representatives from organizations like the National Junior College Athletic Association and Association of College Unions International to help align bowling with other college sports and NCAA regulations.

collegiate bowling

There are four general ways to play the sport of bowling – league, open, tournament and elite.

League bowling has been the backbone of the sport since the ABC formed in 1895. People form groups of up to five called teams and compete on a regular basis (weekly, bi-weekly, monthly) for a specific period of time (weeks, months, year). Leagues set some form of competitive schedule where champions are crowned at the end of the season. These groups come under the auspices of the ABC, WIBC and YABA who offer these bowlers a wide variety of services to make their leagues fun and easy to run.

Open play consists of a variety of unorganized or organized options where people go to the bowling center on their own. Unorganized open play can be friends rolling a couple of games on the spur of the moment. It can be when youth go with their parents for the first time or when a couple goes bowling on a date. It also can be when someone simply wants to practice either alone, with a coach or with others.

Organized open play features activities such as birthday parties, company outings, "glow bowling" or "rock 'n' roll bowling."

Tournaments are more organized activities where competition is at its fiercest. These events can take place over one day, one weekend, one month or over several months. They range from in-center competitions to city, state, regional or national championships to international events where medals are given for representing a bowler's country.

Elite bowling is performed either by top amateurs through programs such as TEAM USA or in the professional ranks through the Professional Bowlers Association and Professional Women's Bowling Association. TEAM USA offers members of ABC, WIBC and YABA the opportunity to represent their country in international competition. PBA and PWBA provide chances to make money not only in competition but through product endorsements and guest appearances.

Bowling truly offers something for everybody. Now, it's time to learn how the sport is played and the way to truly get the most out of the bowling experience no matter how you play the game.

Like any sport, bowling has its own unique places to play the game. They're called bowling centers (or bowling alleys to some people) and without them, there would be no bowling.

They come in sizes from two to 106 lanes. They exist in settings from basements of taverns to being part of large shopping complexes to attached to hotel/casinos. They are located in small towns and large, in central cities and in growing suburbs.

No matter what the differences in size, location or style, all certified bowling centers feature lanes the same length and width and pins the same shape. They are certified each year by the American Bowling Congress and Women's International Bowling Congress as a service to their members. No other sport goes to such lengths to ensure its playing fields are the same from Maine to California, from Washington to Florida, and from Canada to Puerto Rico to U.S. military bases worldwide.

The instructional portion of this book is primarily intended for beginning bowlers, even though experienced bowlers will benefit from its basic principles.

These principles have proven successful during thousands of bowling clinics, videos and televised programs throughout the world. They are the product of more than 30 years of testing and refinement. An individual who wants to improve can learn the game and become a successful competitor simply by understanding and practicing the keys explained here.

Many new bowlers fear they may not be good enough to join a team. The beauty of bowling is any person can compete effectively in a sanctioned league. This is because of the handicap system. The handicap system gives bowlers with lower averages a "head start" by giving them handicap points before the game even starts.

For those who want to learn more advanced bowling techniques and truly excel in the sport, it is strongly recommended obtaining a USA Bowling certified coach or attend a USA Bowling bronze conference. To find one in your area, call USA Bowling at (414)421-9008 or visit **www.bowl.com**.

ABOUT THE PLAYING FIELD

The unique aspect of bowling's playing field is it is essentially the same throughout the world. Thanks to standardized specifications established by the American Bowling Congress and Women's International Bowling Congress, height, width, length and weight for bowling lanes, pins and balls vary little from bowling center to bowling center.

Among these specifications:

•Regulation bowling lanes, constructed out of wood or synthetic products, are essentially 63 feet long. The distance from the foul line to the front pin is 60 feet. The lanes are 41-42 inches wide. The lane approach must be at least 15 feet. Each lane includes spotting markings

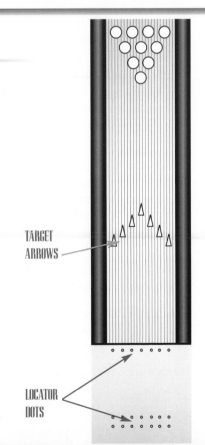

TARGET ARROWS

LOCATOR DOTS

known as locator dots and arrows to help bowlers target their shots.

•Lane dressings or oil, which help protect the lane surface, must contain an ABC/WIBC approved additive and meet minimum content standards.

To ensure these and other standards are met, bowling centers receive an annual certification by local ABC/WIBC representatives. This measurement and inspection of bowling lanes is one way the ABC and WlBC assure members of standard playing conditions.

•The last three feet of the lane is known as the pin deck.

The 10 pins used in the sport are placed in a triangular configuration with each pin being 12 inches apart.

The front pin is called the head or 1 pin. Pins are counted left-to-right by row with the pin

behind and to the left of the head pin called the 2 pin. Behind and right of the head pin is the 3 pin.

Row 3 from left to right are the 4, 5 and 6 pins. The back row has the 7, 8, 9 and 10 pins.

•Pins, made of wood or synthetics, must weigh between 3 pounds, 6 ounces and 3 pounds, 10 ounces at a height of 15 inches.

For just about every sport, one or more pieces of equipment are necessary to participate. In bowling the major piece of equipment is the bowling ball.

The first bowling balls were constructed nearly 7,000 years ago in Egypt and were made of stone. During the 17th, 18th and 19th centuries, balls were made from hard tropical wood or a laminate of different types of wood. In the early 1900s, the hard rubber ball was developed. Today's balls are constructed of rugged plastic polymers with various additives and cores.

A bowling ball is more than a heavy globe with three holes in it. Bowling balls are dynamically balanced and drilled to provide comfort and perform in specific ways on the lane.

The second most important pieces of equipment are your bowling shoes. Bowling shoes are designed to prevent scuff marks on the approach, provide traction and enable a good slide during the release. There are different types of bowling shoes for right-handed and left-handed bowlers.

BOWLING BALL BASICS

A bowling ball is composed of two-major components: the shell and an internal weight block. The shell is the outside covering of the ball. It is hard and durable to withstand landing on the lanes and impacting the pins.

All bowling balls contain an internal weight block. The weight block usually is constructed out of heavy dense materials that will create specific dynamic properties affecting the way a ball will react on the lanes.

Weight blocks vary in size, weights and shapes depending on the different equipment manufacturers. Consult a USA Bowling certified coach and pro shop professional before purchasing any equipment.

Bowling balls are drilled with three holes for the thumb, middle finger and ring finger. The distance between the two finger holes and the thumbhole is known as the span. The distance between the two finger holes is known as the bridge.

All bowling balls are 27 inches in circumference and approximately 8.5 inches in diameter. The weight of a bowling ball will range from six to 16 pounds. According to ABC/WIBC regulations, a bowling ball may not weigh more than 16 pounds. There is no minimum weight for a bowling ball.

There are various markings on the outside of a bowling ball. Usually you will find the logo of the manufacturer, the brand name of the ball and a serial number. Some bowlers also have their names engraved on a bowling ball. On a house ball (provided by a bowling center), the weight of the ball will be marked above the finger holes.

Note: If you use house balls and do not have a bowling ball yet, remember that every ball has its own serial number. If you find a ball that works well for you, remember the serial number so you can find it the next time you bowl.

BALL GRIP

Holes are drilled in bowling balls by pro shop professionals located either within the bowling center or at a separate facility. A good ball driller is a skilled specialist who will work with you to customize a ball that

CONVENTIONAL GRIP

FINGERTIP GRIP

will fit your hand perfectly and complement the way you bowl.

Having a proper grip is the most important part of a bowler's game. A proper grip will allow a bowler to learn proper form and technique and minimize the risk of injury.

FIT OF FINGER/THUMB HOLES

You want the finger and thumbholes to be snug enough so you won't drop the ball, yet loose enough to afford a smooth release. The thumbhole should be a little looser than the finger holes, since the thumb drops out first during the release.

Note: If the holes are too big, you can place a strip of tape in the back of the holes to make them smaller. You can do this according to the weather. Usually, your hands are somewhat larger when it's warm outside and smaller when it's cold.

You may have heard people mention thumb and finger pitch. This refers to how the holes are drilled in relation to the center of the ball. A skilled ball driller will make sure that the pitch of the thumb and fingers are perfect for you and your game.

FIT IN THE HAND

The distance between the two finger holes (bridge) should be about a quarter inch. The distance between the thumb hole and finger holes (span) depends upon the size of your hand and which type of grip you use. (We'll cover the types of grips shortly.) Comfort is the key. Notice the web of skin between your thumb and index finger. With a properly fitted ball the web should be neither taut nor slack.

TYPES OF GRIPS

There are two basic types of grips: conventional and fingertip.

With a conventional grip, the fingers enter up to the second knuckle of the hand. In the fingertip grip, the fingers enter only up to the first knuckle.

For new bowlers and those who bowl once a week or less, the conventional grip is the grip of choice.

If you are a frequent bowler and truly want to excel in the sport, adopt a fingertip grip. This is the grip most professionals use.

The fingertip grip will encourage a quicker, smoother thumb and finger release than the conventional release.

BALL COVER

When referring to the cover of the ball, it means the texture or finish. You have probably noticed that some balls have a dull finish while others are shiny.

The major factor in determining how soon a ball will hook is surface roughness.

Sanded balls are dull and scratchy, like the surface of an old weather-beaten car. Polished balls are bright and shiny, like the surface of a newly waxed car.

On the lane, balls with different covers will act differently. A dull, sanded ball will bite into the surface of the lane, provide earlier traction and hook more. A shiny, polished ball will skid more and hook less.

If the lane conditions are dry, you may be getting more hook than you want. Switching to a shinier, polished ball will help reduce this hook.

If the lane conditions are oily, your ball may not be getting enough traction to hook at all.

Using a dull, sanded ball instead will increase traction and your hooking potential.

Remember:

Dull, Sanded Ball
- Better Traction on Lane.
- More Hook.
- Use on Oily Lanes.

Shiny, Polished Ball
- Less Traction on Lane.
- More Skidding and Less Hook.
- Use on Dry Lanes.

BALL WEIGHT IN GENERAL

As we mentioned earlier, balls range in weight from six to 16 pounds. Which weight is correct for you? A general rule of thumb is to use the heaviest ball you can control without sacrificing accuracy or ball speed.

When you go to a bowling center or pro shop, try handling balls of different weight. If a ball is too light, you will be able to toss it around easily. If a ball is too heavy, you will feel weighed down and off balance handling it.

BOWLING SHOES

There is a difference between the house bowling shoes you rent at the control counter of a bowling center and those you purchase for personal use.

The soles of the shoes you rent are leather on both the right and left feet. Leather soles enable your feet to slide easier when you get to the foul line. The heels are made of white rubber to prevent leaving marks on the approach.

When you get your own personal shoes, only one of the shoes will have a leather sole. For a right-handed bowler, the sole of the left shoe will be leather. This is the foot on which you slide toward the foul line. The right sole will be rubber to give you traction. (Sometimes the toe of this shoe will have leather on the bottom to help your foot slide sideways in back of the body easier.)

For a left-handed bowler, the sole of the right shoe will be leather. This is the foot on which you slide toward to foul line. The left sole will be rubber to give you traction. (Sometimes the toe of this shoe will have leather on the bottom to help your foot slide sideways in back of the body easier.)

Note: In this section the basics of bowling balls and shoes have been covered. For those who want to learn more about how using different balls can improve your game, talk to a USA Bowling certified coach. To find one in your area, call 414/421-9008.

BOWLING AIDS

There are many types of bowling aids for the wrist, palm and fingers which could help the bowler improve, and there are others in the form of protective aids. Bowling aids are individual items which bowlers may purchase, other than bags, balls and shoes.

There are many different types of wrist products designed to keep the wrist firm so the bowler doesn't have to worry about keeping it stiff or straight.

The glove type aids often have cushions in the palm to help the bowler place the fingers and thumb in the ball at the same depth each time, keep in contact with the ball throughout delivery and keep pressure off the fingers in the stance. Although many think the aids will help improve scores, the greatest asset is to help keep the hand position straighter because a glove can make a bowler feel a wrong movement or could help change a backup bowler to a hook bowler. It can't completely solve the wrong wrist movement but it does make the bowler think about the position of the wrist at point of release.

Rosin is available for the finger and thumb to help the bowler better grip the ball. There is rosin which provides stickiness for bowlers with smooth hands, and smooth solutions for bowlers with sweaty or sticky hands.

Protective aids, such as nylon type material, are applied to the fingers or thumb where a cut or tear appears, or to a potential callous. Nylon and cotton type aids are used to protect an open blister. Usually this is used with a type of new skin or collodion, something sticky that you can put the gauze on so it will adhere to the skin and eliminate friction from the ball.

Thumb irritation is a common ailment for bowlers who compete often during each week. A bowler with a bad irritation or callus might check the pitch of the thumb hole. A change in pitch might alleviate the problem. Calluses which develop over a period of time might be sanded down with an emery cloth or board.

Other bowling aids include towels to help keep hands and bowling balls dry and clean, tape to adjust finger grip width and wire brushes to clean bowling shoes. Check with your pro shop professional to best determine your individual needs.

PROMOTING SAFE AND COURTEOUS BOWLING

You are no doubt anxious to start improving your bowling skills. Before that, however, are some basic points that will make your visits to the bowling center safe and enjoyable from the beginning.

First are some safety tips to make your visits to the bowling center fun and safe. Then there are some stretching and loosening exercises that will limber your body prior to bowling, promote smoother physical movement and help prevent injury.

Finally, there will be a few basics of bowling etiquette. Remembering these do's and don'ts will prevent embarrassment and possible hurt feelings.

Even though as many as 90 million people bowl a year, the chance of injury on the lanes actually is very small compared to other sports, but accidents still happen. Bowling is a sport. As with all other sports, injury may result if basic safety practices are not followed.

AVOID MOISTURE ON YOUR SHOES

Moisture is probably your No. 1 enemy when bowling. The smooth rubber and leather on bowling shoe soles get sticky when even slightly wet. This can be treacherous on the approach.

Always use bowling shoes on the lanes. On rainy or snowy days, don't leave the bowling area more than necessary. Be sure to keep food and beverages out of the bowling area. Instead, enjoy refreshments in the concourse, lounge and snack bar areas. And watch where you walk whenever you leave the bowling area. Remember, the moisture you deposit on the approach is a hazard for your teammates as well as you.

Sometimes, new bowling shoes stick to the approach even when they are dry. Don't make the mistake of many bowlers and use baby powder on your soles. This can make them too slippery and will also create a hazard for other bowlers. Instead, use a knife and some sandpaper to round and smooth the leading edge of the heel of your sliding shoe. In extreme cases, placing a piece of Teflon tape to the leading edge of your heel will correct the problem.

BOWLING BALL SAFETY

It sounds silly to say, "don't drop the ball on your foot," but many great bowlers accidentally have done just that. A bowling ball is a smooth, heavy object that can easily slip from your

grasp if you're not careful. Before you pick up a bowling ball, always dry your hands with a towel or use the air blowers on the ball return.

When you pick up a ball from the return, grasp the ball from the sides. This prevents pinched fingers in case another ball comes zipping out.

Don't put your fingers in the ball when you are picking it up and carrying it. Conserve the strength in your throwing hand and fingers for actual bowling. Instead, after you pick up the ball, cradle it in your opposite arm.

Be careful when lifting your bowling bag. Many bowlers carry two or more bowling balls in their bags. With the addition of shoes, wrist aids, other equipment and the weight of the bag itself, the combined weight can be over 50 pounds. When lifting your bag out of the car, keep your back straight, bend at the knees and waist, and use the big muscles of your legs to lift. Also, keep the weight of the bag close to your body. Find a bowling ball bag with wheels.

COMMON SENSE IS THE KEY

Obviously, the best way to prevent injuries is to remain aware of what is going on around you and use simple common sense.

After throwing a shot, make sure to walk back on your side of the approach. Some people tend to watch their shots as they walk backward from the foul line. Drifting to the right or left is a good way to get in another person's way.

BASIC WARM-UP EXERCISES TO PREVENT INJURY

If people viewed bowling as a sport requiring proper strength and conditioning, the number of bowling-related injuries would probably be significantly reduced. While some injuries are caused by accidents, many others are the result of strain and stress on the body that builds up over time. This is called microtrauma. In bowling, microtrauma builds up in the shoulder, elbow, wrist and hand.

The principal cause of micro-trauma is lack of pre-bowling warm-up. Performing some simple warm-up exercises just before bowling will limber your muscles and joints, prepare your body for maximum physical performance and help prevent injury.

The following loosening up exercises are designed to especially limber those areas used the most during bowling. It is recommend performing three sets of five repetitions for each exercise.

These exercises are most effective when they are performed once or twice daily, and especially just before bowling.

Note: The following exercises have been taken from the YABA coaching manual *Beyond the Beginner*, by Fred Borden.

QUADRICEPS

Balance on one leg while grasping foot of other leg and stretch it back to the opposite buttock. Alternate with other leg. This will stretch the front leg muscles.

TRICEPS

Lift elbow of one arm over head (with rest of arm lowered). Grasp elbow with opposite hand and pull gently toward middle of head. Alternate with other arm.

FOREARM EXTENDERS

Extend arm with hand bent downward at the wrist. Grasp fingers with other hand. Pull toward body. Repeat with other hand.

FOREARM FLEXORS

Extend arm, with palm facing out and hand bent upward at the wrist. Grasp fingers with other hand. Pull toward body. Repeat with other hand.

NECK/SHOULDER STRETCH

Bend head down. Slowly rotate head in a clockwise, then counterclockwise, motion.

NECK STRETCH

Move chin toward Adam's apple until you can feel tension on back of neck.

CALF STRETCH

Balance balls of feet on stair (or step to approach and ball return). Lower and raise body at the ankle.

SIDE STRETCH

Extend right arm over head, while keeping other arm at side. Bend sideways at the waist toward left side. Alternate with other side.

KNEE/THIGH STRETCH

Place your left leg in back and your right leg in front of your body. By bending your right knee and extending your left leg, shift your weight forward and hold. Alternate leg position and repeat.

ACHILLES STRETCH

Place palms up against a wall. Place your left leg in back and your right leg in front of your body. Stretch out your left leg while bending your right knee until you feel tension, and hold. Repeat with legs alternated.

TOE TOUCH

Cross legs. Bend body at waist, moving fingers as close as comfortable toward toes. Hold. Alternate position of feet and repeat.

When you go to bowl, you expect to have a good time. That means enjoying the companionship of your friends, relaxing in the pleasant atmosphere of the bowling center and getting some good exercise while developing your skills.

Nothing can spoil a great attitude faster than having an annoying person next to you. You have a right to be treated with respect. If you are like most people, your free time is rare and therefore valuable. You expect to be able to enjoy yourself during the occasional breaks from your busy schedule.

Respect works both ways. You must first treat others with respect in order to receive it.

WHO BOWLS FIRST?

When you get up to bowl, and there are two people on either side of you, who should bowl first? The general rule is: the first one up should go first. If there is any question who was the first to get up, the person to the right should bowl first.

DON'T WAIT: JUST DO IT!

Another guideline to remember is that once you are lined up in your stance, don't wait, take a deep breath, then go. Many people get in the stance, fidget for awhile until they feel they have it right, then stare in fixation at the pins for a minute or more.

You can't stare the pins down! If you want to knock them down, you have to throw the ball!

During fast-paced competition people get annoyed quickly with a person who hesitates in the stance. Moreover, hesitation does not promote a proper mental game and makes your muscles tense. People who hesitate in the stance tend to "over-think" and end up getting "psyched out." The time for thinking about a shot is before you line up in the stance. Once you step up on the approach, the time for thinking is over. Just do it!

And if the lanes are crowded and others are waiting to bowl, don't wait at the foul line to see what you are going to get.

Adopting these guidelines will help promote a fast-paced game and make the evening more exciting.

PRACTICE RESTRAINT

Obviously, in the heat of competition, emotions and enthusiasm run high. And that's one of the things that makes bowling such a great sport.

Just make sure your enthusiasm doesn't hinder or irritate those around you. Obviously, your enthusiasm about making three strikes in a row will not be appreciated by those next to you if you run over into their lane whooping and hollering.

Be especially considerate toward your teammates. Part of the camaraderie of friendship is taking – or giving – a little ribbing from time to time. But don't get carried away and make jokes at the expense of others. Again, treat people the way you would want to be treated.

Bowling is a wholesome family sport, so don't use profanity in the bowling center. Do have a good time, but try not to be overly loud or rowdy.

Avoid negative mental attitudes. Throwing temper tantrums or becoming glum and moody will do more than aggravate your teammates. Negative mental attitudes will adversely affect your performance.

TAKE CARE OF YOUR BOWLING CENTER

Caring for a bowling center is everyone's responsibility, not just the proprietor's. Remember:

the condition of a bowling center reflects on the public perception of bowlers and bowling as a sport.

If you smoke, be careful not to burn furnishings and floor coverings. Put chewing gum where it belongs. Clean up your spills and dispose of all trash in waste receptacles.

When you are visiting other bowling centers, respect their rules. Though the rules may not be the same as you are used to, complying with them is simply a matter of good manners. Remember: "When in Rome ..."

Imagine a sprinter dropping down into the track blocks preparing to run, a baseball player getting up to bat, a golfer lining up for a shot or a football lineman dropping into a three-point stance.

In each of these examples, an athlete is preparing the body to perform. Though the positions vary according to the sport, each athlete assumes a stance that will translate into top performance when it comes time to move.

In bowling, a correct stance is just as important as in any other sport. A bowler is an athlete preparing to perform a series of precise athletic movements. The body must be located at the correct spot in a well-balanced, comfortable position.

This section covers the two basic aspects of the stance: where to line up and how to line up.

If you are a new bowler, the points covered may seem like a lot to remember at first. After

the first few times, though, you'll notice that a correct stance simply feels right. Soon, your body will naturally assume a proper stance without any conscious thought.

WHERE TO LINE UP

There are two things to consider when determining where to line up: distance from the lane and positioning to the right or left.

On the approach, there are marks to help you determine where to line up: the foul line and locator dots.

DISTANCE FROM FOUL LINE

All instruction in this guide will be based on utilizing the classic four-step delivery.

As a general rule, a person five feet tall would want to line up on the second set of locator dots from the foul line. This will vary, though, according to your height. A taller person will want to line up farther

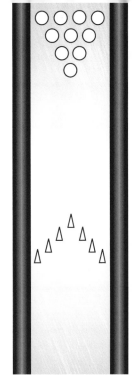

1. Line up facing away from the lane with your heels approximately two inches from the foul line.

2. If you are right-handed, start with your right foot and take 4 1/2 brisk steps. If you are left-handed, start with your left foot and take 4 1/2 brisk steps. The four steps take into account the four steps for the approach. The extra half step is for the slide at the end. It will also give you some leeway so you don't go over the foul line.

3. Pivot on the foot in front of you so you are facing the lane. This is where you should line up.

LINING UP TO THE RIGHT OR LEFT

If you are right-handed, line up with the inside of the left foot an inch or so to the left of the center dot. If you are left-handed, line up with the inside of the right foot an inch or so to the right of the center dot.

When practicing, move right and left in the stance one inch at a time until you find the spot that is perfect for you. This is the basic position where you will line up when making strikes (trying to knock down all 10 pins at the same time).

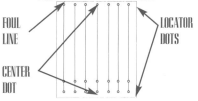

FOUL LINE

LOCATOR DOTS

CENTER DOT

away than a shorter person. This is because a taller person has a longer stride.

Here is a simple method to precisely determine how far away to line up.

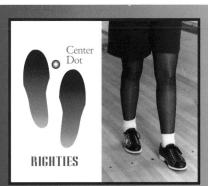

Center Dot

RIGHTIES

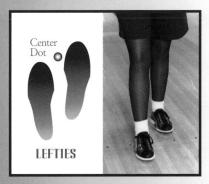

Center Dot

LEFTIES

BODY POSITION: WAIST DOWN
Feet

If you bowl right-handed, position your right foot about three to five inches in back of your left foot. This will give you a better base. Also, it will help you start easier during the approach, since you will be moving your right foot first.

If you are left-handed, position your left foot about three to five inches in back of your right foot.

Knees

When you line up in the stance, flex your knees slightly. After all, you are an athlete preparing to execute a series of fluid movements. Avoid locking your knee joints. Instead, bend and relax them for balance.

How far? It is recommended you tilt your knees forward 10-15 degrees so they extend out toward the toes four to six inches.

How would you bend your knees if you were catching a bag of potatoes dropped from a truck? This is a good mental picture of how to position yourself.

Be sure to keep your knees flexed throughout the approach without straightening up.

BODY POSITION: WAIST UP
Spine

When it comes time to bowl, you are going to be moving forward. To help prepare yourself, the weight of your body should be positioned forward.

Tilt your spine forward approximately 15 degrees. Make sure you maintain this position throughout the approach and delivery.

Shoulders

When you bowl, the weight of the ball is on one side of your body. It's only natural that the height of one shoulder will be a little lower than the other.

If you bowl right-handed, let your right shoulder drop a couple inches lower than the left. If you bowl left-handed, allow your left shoulder to drop a couple inches lower than the right.

It's been said we could all bowl better if our eyes were on top of our shoulder. Then we could see the path of the ball precisely. We can still develop good mental pictures of this. We call the path the ball takes down the lane the Target Line or the Line in Your Mind.

When you bowl, imagine a three-foot arrow resting on your shoulder. Align this three-foot arrow with the target line.

Arms

Make sure the elbow of your bowling arm is resting against your side when holding the ball. The other hand should help cradle and support the ball in the stance.

WHERE TO HOLD THE BOWLING BALL

You've probably noticed that some bowlers hold the ball at chest level, while other bowlers hold it at hip level or below. Both of these positions – and any in between – are correct.

Where you hold the ball depends upon how fast you get to the foul line in the approach. The faster you are, the lower you hold the ball. This will help synchronize the arm swing to your steps during the approach.

A slow bowler should hold the ball at chest level. A medium speed bowler should hold the

lefties

CHEST LEVEL:
SLOWER TO THE FOUL LINE

WAIST LEVEL:
FASTER TO THE FOUL LINE

ball at waist level. A fast bowler should hold the ball below the waist.

Experiment with different positions until you find the one that is right for you.

HOW TO HOLD THE BOWLING BALL

In the stance, the weight of the ball should rest against the palm of your bowling hand. As mentioned earlier, the other hand should help support the weight of the bowling ball. The little finger of each hand should touch.

You may have a question about what fingers go in what holes. Your thumb goes into the hole that is larger than the other two holes and is apart from them. Place your middle finger and ring finger in the other holes.

When placing your hand in the ball, it's important to always put your fingers in first and then your thumb. This will promote a smooth release since the thumb comes out of the ball before the fingers when delivering the ball down the lane. You'll learn later of different ways to position the ball in your hand, but for now keep your hand underneath the ball with the weight of the ball in the palm of your hand.

Another way to visualize this is to imagine the face of a clock around your bowling ball. If you

are right-handed, your thumb should be in the 10 o'clock position. If you are left-handed, place your thumb in the 2 o'clock position.

It is important to maintain this hand position throughout the approach delivery and release. When you throw the ball, imagine that you are shaking hands with the pins.

Wrist

Keep your wrist straight during the release. You may notice that some advanced bowlers cup their wrist to give the ball more spin, or break the wrist to make the ball go straighter. This is an advanced technique you should only try after mastering the basics.

Make sure your wrist remains in the same position throughout the approach and delivery.

BOWLING BALANCE

If you follow all the guidelines we have just explained, you should feel relaxed, balanced and natural in the stance. When in the stance, your weight should be balanced on the balls of your feet. Just before you begin your approach, rock back on your heels very slightly, then forward as you begin to take your first step. This rocking motion should not be noticeable to the eye but just enough so that you can feel it.

A proper approach combines agility, speed, form, coordination, timing and accuracy. All muscles in the body function in unison to send a bowling ball on its precise course to the pins.

Mastering the approach first takes knowledge. Then it takes lots of practice to train the muscles to perform what the mind already knows. A successful approach occurs when the body and mind work as one in a free-flowing series of coordinated movements.

The most common approach is the four step. Each footstep will be numbered, then related to the position of the bowling ball at the end of each step.

There are five separate positions. The first is the stance position. It is called the 0:0 position.

The position of the right foot is numbered 0 and shown in relation to the ball position, which is also numbered 0.

STEP ONE: POSITION 1:1

During the first step, the right foot steps forward as the right arm pushes the ball out and down toward the right foot

simultaneously. At the end of the first step, the ball should be poised above the right foot. The left hand should continue to help support the ball throughout this step.

Note: If you bowl left-handed, move your left foot forward as the left hand pushes the ball out toward the lane and over the foot.

Two points are important to remember during this step:

1. Make sure the leg and arm start at the same time. If the ball and foot don't end up in the 1:1 position simultaneously, your timing will be off throughout the approach.

2. Move the ball straight out toward the lane so it ends up over your right foot.

Often this is referred to as the pushaway, because you should push the ball out toward the lane and down toward the floor.

STEP TWO: POSITION 2:2

During the second step the left foot moves forward as the ball arcs down. The left hand should leave the ball at the

| THE STANCE | STEP ONE | STEP TWO | STEP THREE |

beginning of the step. At the end of the second step, the ball should end up beside the right calf.

Note: For left-handers, during the second step the right foot moves forward as the ball arcs down. The right hand should leave the ball at the beginning of the step. At the end of the second step, the ball should end up beside the left calf.

STEP THREE POSITION 3:3

During the third step the right foot moves forward as the ball arcs back to the highest point of the arm swing. This should be about shoulder height.

Note: Left-handers should move your left foot forward as the ball arcs back to the height of the back swing.

STEP FOUR: POSITION 4:4

During the fourth step the left foot should step forward into the slide as the ball arcs down. At the end of the fourth step, the ball should be in the lowest part of the arm swing. The right arm should be pointed directly at the floor.

Note: If you bowl left-handed, move your right foot forward and plant for the slide while the ball arcs down.

After the fourth step you should continue through the release and follow-through without hesitation. As the ball starts down during the fourth step, your right foot should slide sideways in back of your left leg. Simultaneously, you should "sit down" or lower your knees slightly and position your weight slightly back so you end up in a comfortable sitting position with the lower body and the spine tilted 15 degrees forward.

Note: Left-handers' left foot should slide sideways in back of the right leg.

Make sure you do not slide over the foul line during the fourth step. If you slide over the foul line during competition (and release the ball), you receive no points for the shot.

AVOID DRIFTING

Be careful not to drift to the right or left with your feet during the approach. Drifting is another major cause of inaccuracy. Check where your feet are located after a shot. You should end up with your feet within one or two boards of where you lined up in the stance.

| STEP FOUR | THE RELEASE | THE FOLLOW-THROUGH |

The locator dots where you line up are lined up with the locator dots beside the foul line. This means if you line up in the stance with your feet between the center dot, you should end up with your feet between the center dot at the foul line.

As with an inaccurate arm swing, drifting is usually caused by improper timing. If the arm swing is not properly timed to the footsteps, the body will not be balanced properly. This results in the body drifting right or left. Review the keys to proper timing if you experience drifting. Remember, accuracy is not possible unless the arm swing is straight.

THE FIVE STEP APPROACH

You may have heard about the five-step approach. The five-step approach is the same as the four-step approach except there is an initial "getting started" baby step at the beginning. The ball does not move from the stance position during this initial step.

If you bowl right-handed, this small first step will be with the left foot. If you bowl left-handed, the step will be with the right foot.

After the baby step, the five-step approach is the same as the four-step approach.

Note: If you use the five-step approach, make sure to give yourself more room from the foul line to allow for the extra baby step.

lefties

TARGETING - WHERE TO AIM

You are probably anxious to practice and want to know where to aim for a strike. Notice there are seven arrows on the lane. These are called target arrows. The arrows are numbered from right-to-left if you bowl right-handed, or from left-to-right if you bowl left-handed.

For now, aim for the second target arrow. The ball should hook between the 1 pin and 3 pin. This area is called the strike pocket, because this is the best place to hit the pins to make a strike. For left-handed bowlers, the strike pocket is between the 1 and 2 pins.

lefties

If your first shot consistently misses to the right, it is recommended to move your starting position one to two boards to the right on the approach. (*Note:* do not change your target on the lane). If it misses a little to the left, move a little to the left.

Using the arrows is a major part of the four ways to target your shots. There is spot bowling, line bowling, area bowling and pin bowling.

SPOT BOWLING

Generally, a spot bowler uses a target arrow as a guide to the 1-3 pocket (1-2 for left-handers). The 1-3 (1-2) pocket is the ultimate goal. The target arrow or spot is only a guide to the pocket. Merely hitting the spot, however, does not insure the ball rolling into the 1-3 (1-2) pocket. That's why it is important to sight line each delivery. Draw an imaginary line with the shoulder, target arrow and pins included. Face toward the pins, walk fairly straight and swing in line with the target. A bowler does not have to use an arrow as the target. Many select a spot

somewhere closer to the foul line or out on the lane.

LINE BOWLING

Line bowling is a combination of pin and spot bowling. Pick a starting spot, a spot at the foul line, a spot out on the lane and then check the 1-3 or 1-2 pocket. While going through delivery, the bowler sometimes shifts glances from one target to the next. Always look at the target. It is difficult to move the eyes from one target to another. There are variations of line bowling. Some bowlers draw a line from the 1-3 or 1-2 pocket to the target arrow only. Some draw the line from the bowling shoulder to the target arrow only.

AREA BOWLING

If the second arrow is the target to the 1-3 or 1-2 pocket, look at the target and one board to the left and one board to the right, giving a three-board area in width. Then line up the shoulder with the target, walk fairly straight and swing straight. The three-board area will provide some margin of error but should keep the ball near the 1-3 or 1-2 pocket. Selecting a specific board or boards as a sight line also can be used effectively. That also holds true for the other illustrations.

PIN BOWLING

Look at the pins and draw an imaginary line between the spot of delivery to a point on the pin setup, usually the 1-3

or 1-2 pocket. The line is the route over which the ball should travel. Few bowlers today look at the pins because it is easier to hit a target 15 feet away accurately than to hit a target 60 feet away. That's why it is suggested to use the arrows as a target, regardless of what type of bowling.

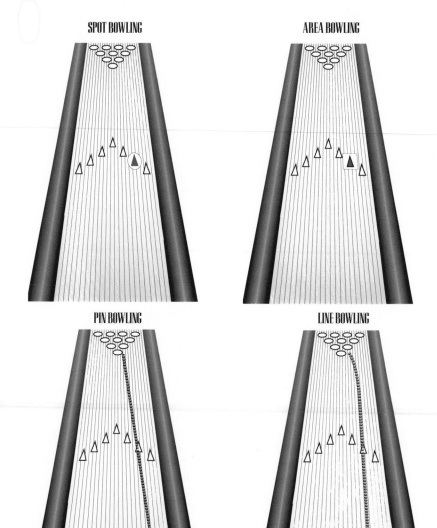

SPOT BOWLING

AREA BOWLING

PIN BOWLING

LINE BOWLING

Talking about the arm swing really means talking about accuracy. Keeping the arm on line and developing a consistent arm swing are the two keys to accuracy.

Notice the emphasis placed on consistency. Developing consistency in your game is the first requirement to becoming a truly great bowler.

2. Arc the ball back between 5 and 6 o'clock during the back swing.

3. Arc the ball forward between the 12 and 1 o'clock position during the forward swing and delivery.

If you bowl left-handed, during the arm swing you want to:

THE ARM SWING

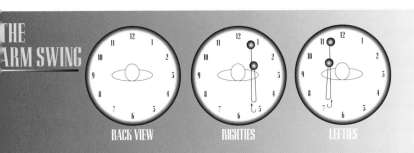

BACK VIEW   RIGHTIES   LEFTIES

Consistency is more important in the arm swing than in any other area of bowling. As you will soon learn, where you line up in the stance will vary. How you hold the bowling ball may vary. But your arm swing should never vary.

Arm swing here is analyzed from two views – back and the side.

THE ARM SWING: BACK VIEW

To visualize the front-to-back view, imagine you are standing inside the face of a clock. Directly in front of you would be 12 o'clock. Just to the right of you would be 1 o'clock. Directly behind you would be 6 o'clock, and just to the right of this would be 5 o'clock.

If you bowl right handed, during the arm swing you want to:

1. Push the ball out between 12 and 1 o'clock during the pushaway.

1. Push the ball out between 12 and 11 o'clock during the pushaway.

2. Arc the ball back between 7 and 6 o'clock during the back swing.

3. Arc the ball forward between the 12 and 11 o'clock position during the forward swing and delivery.

ARM IN = BALL OUT

For a right-handed player, a ball that begins in a 10-11 o'clock position will generally arc away from the body to a 4-5 o'clock position at the height of the back swing. Moving the ball forward will take the arm swing back to 10-11 o'clock pulling your shot left of your target.

For a left-handed player, a ball that begins in a 1-2 o'clock position will generally arc away from the body to a 7-8 o'clock

lefties

position at the height of the back swing. Moving the ball forward will result in pulling the shot left of the target.

ARM OUT = BALL IN

For a right-handed bowler, you begin your stance in a 2-3 o'clock position, the ball at the height of the back swing will generally tuck in behind the back in a 7-8 o'clock position. The ball moving forward will end in the beginning 2-3 o'clock area pulling the shot right of the target.

Left-handed bowlers would have the same thing happen starting from the 9-10 o'clock stance position, behind the back to the 4-5 and moving forward to 9-10.

THE ARM SWING: SIDE VIEW

All footsteps have been numbered to show how the movements of the feet correspond to a properly timed arm swing.

Notice that the back swing goes up to about shoulder height. It is important to keep the height of your arm swing consistent. This will promote consistent timing.

ARM IN = BALL OUT   ARM OUT = BALL IN

From the back swing, the arm arcs down toward the floor, then back up and through to the finish position. Imagine an airplane coming in for a landing, then taking off again just before touching the ground. This is what a proper forward swing resembles.

Notice points of thumb release and finger release also are shown. The thumb releases at the lowest point of the arm swing, just after the fourth step. The fingers release as you begin arcing up toward the finish position. Since the fingers are on the side of the ball, this translates into sideways spin and hook potential.

In the finish position the arm should be raised with the hand pointing toward the ceiling.

ARM SWING SIDE VIEW

FIRST THREE STEPS - BACK SWING

STEP #3

STANCE POSITION

STEP #2

STEP #1

FOURTH STEP - DELIVERY SWING

FOLLOW THROUGH

STEP #4

THUMB RELEASE

FINGER RELEASE

Some new bowlers have difficulty with the release. Always check the grip and weight of the ball. Perhaps this is because there are many different types of releases. A beginning bowler will often become confused, or try to adopt more advanced releases before mastering the simple ones.

Also, new bowlers often fear they will drop the bowling ball prematurely. The forward momentum of the bowling ball, however, usually keeps it firmly against the hand until it's time to release it.

When performed properly, the release should occur naturally. The holes on a bowling ball are drilled in such a way to encourage a good release with the thumb and fingers releasing out of the holes at the proper time.

REVIEW OF SUITCASE RELEASE

As mentioned earlier, to perform a suitcase (handshake) release, put the thumb in the 10 o'clock "handshake position" in the stance. Then maintain this position throughout the approach and release.

If you bowl left-handed, put your thumb in the 2 o'clock position and maintain it throughout the approach and release.

Develop a mental picture of reaching out and shaking hands with the second target arrow. This should help keep the thumb in the correct position.

REVIEW OF RELEASE TIMING

If you are holding the ball naturally and your thumb and fingers fit comfortably in the holes (not too tight and not too

loose), the thumb should drop out of the ball at the end of the fourth step. This is the lowest point of the delivery swing.

After the thumb releases, the fingers remain in the ball while lifting out and up toward the finish position. Since the fingers are on the side of the ball, this natural lifting action will impart sideways spin on the ball.

MAINTAIN YOUR HAND POSITION

Some bowlers try to force the hook by turning the hand up over the ball at the moment of release. It is important to maintain the same hand position from the moment you line up in stance until you end up in the finish position.

MAINTAIN YOUR WRIST POSITION

Earlier three types of wrist positions were mentioned: broken, straight and cupped. It is recommended bowlers use a straight wrist. What is important, however, is to make sure the wrist remains in the same

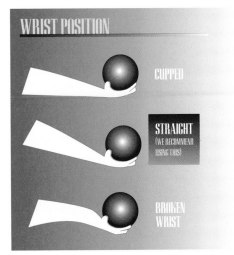

WRIST POSITION

CUPPED

STRAIGHT
(WE RECOMMEND USING THIS)

BROKEN WRIST

position in the stance and throughout the approach, release and follow-through.

THE STRAIGHT BALL

To bowl a straight ball, point your thumb straight up toward the ceiling, (the 12 o'clock position) in the stance. Maintain this position throughout the approach, release and follow-through.

During the slide, the thumb should release from the ball first. As the fingers lift out and up, the ball will simply roll from the fingers and onto the lane. This promotes a good rolling action on the lane.

Note: Since with a straight ball there will be little if any hook on the ball, right-handed bowlers will want to line up a few boards farther to the right in the stance.

Left-handed bowlers will want to line up a few boards farther to the left.

Although a straight delivery is more accurate than a suitcase delivery, keep in mind your percentage of strikes will be lower. This is because there is no hook on the ball and it will deflect sharply when it hits the strike pocket. A straight ball is great for picking up spares.

THE FINISH POSITION

Many people wonder why the finish position is so important. After all, the ball has already been released and is on its way down the lane. There is nothing more that a bowler can do to influence the outcome.

The reason why the finish position is important is balance and help promoting a correct follow-through.

Think about throwing a football. If a quarterback's hands stopped at the moment the football was released, speed, distance and accuracy would be sacrificed. If a tennis player stopped the arm an instant after connecting, the tennis ball probably wouldn't clear the net.

A correct follow-through and finish position will help you maintain accuracy, body balance and consistent success.

THE SLIDE – RIGHTIES

THE SLIDE – LEFTIES

THE SLIDE

As you will recall, at the end of the fourth step the left foot plants for the slide. At the same time the right foot should slide sideways behind the body.

If you are left-handed, plant the right foot for the slide while you slide the left foot behind your body.

Moving the foot in back of the body does three things: it helps move the hip inside to allow more clearance for the bowling ball as it moves past. It provides a broader base to promote better balance during the release and follow-through. And it shifts the weight of the body toward the side opposite the bowling ball for better balance.

Also, lower your hips as if starting to sit a little more during the slide. This promotes better ball delivery onto the lane and also gives you better balance.

THE FOLLOW-THROUGH

Two main points are important to remember during the follow-through:

1. Lift the arm out and up.

2. Keep the body down.

As the ball rolls from your fingers, your arm should continue to arc upwards toward the ceiling. Also, the hand should remain aligned with the target line that the ball will follow down the lane. In the case of a strike ball, your hand would be pointed at the second target arrow.

At the same time, the body should be kept low. This does not mean to bend down. Instead, lower your hips and shift the weight of your body back slightly. When performed properly, it feels comfortable, like sitting back in a chair.

Simply keep your spine tilted 15 degrees forward, flex your knees and let the ball roll right off your fingers as you lift up toward the ceiling.

In the perfect finish position, your head, knee and toe should be aligned in a straight line

THE FOLLOW-THROUGH – RIGHTIES

THE FOLLOW-THROUGH – LEFTIES

perpendicular to the floor. Viewed from the side, the arm should continue arcing upward after ball release. The angle of the spine should be the same as it was in the stance. The knees have flexed further to complement a better delivery of the ball onto the lane.

Looking at this from back to front, for a right-handed bowler the right arm should end up at approximately the 1 o'clock position, with the left leg at 6 o'clock, the right leg at 7 o'clock and the head at 12 o'clock.

For a left-handed bowler the left arm should end up at approximately the 11 o'clock position, with the right leg at 6 o'clock, the left leg at 5 o'clock and the head at 12 o'clock.

You have probably noticed the surface of a lane looks very shiny. At times your bowling ball may come back with an oily ring around it. This is because lane dressing is regularly applied to a lane. The dressing helps protect the wood surface. It also allows the ball to initially skid on the lane surface before hooking and rolling into the pins.

As soon as the oil dressing is applied to a lane it begins to evaporate. How fast the dressing evaporates depends upon how much the lane is being used, overhead lighting, the porosity of the wood, the type of dressing and other factors. Lane conditioning is important because the amount of dressing on a lane determines how your ball will react during a shot.

You may have noticed during a game that even though you were doing everything correct, you consistently missed to the right or left of the head pin. The reason was probably because there was more or less dressing on the lane than the last time you bowled.

The amount of dressing is not the only consideration. Where the dressing is located is also important. The condition of the lane itself is also a factor. If it has been some time since the lanes were refinished, areas have probably become old and worn. All these factors play a role on what your ball does once it leaves your fingers.

CONSISTENCY COMES FIRST

To determine the condition of the lane and adjust accordingly, you first must be able to determine if your physical game and timing feel proper. This means your physical game must be consistent. Adjusting to lane conditions is possible only if:

1. You have an accurate, consistent arm swing.

2. Your arm swing is timed properly with your feet movements.

3. The release has been mastered and is the same every time.

4. You walk straight to the foul line without drifting more than a board or two right or left.

Once you have developed consistency in your physical game, it is time to start considering the condition of the lane and how to adjust.

LANE CONDITIONS

There are three basic types of lane conditions: oily, medium and dry. Think of these conditions as colors spread out on the lane: dry as red, medium as white and oily as blue. As soon as you get up to bowl, try to determine which of these three conditions exist.

Look at the lane. Can you detect patches of lane dressing? Or are there dry, worn patches where the dressing has evaporated? Check your ball when it comes back. Is there a telltale oily ring around it, or is it fairly dry?

HOW LANE CONDITIONS AFFECT YOUR GAME

Lane conditions affect the performance of your ball on the lane. This is why it is necessary to learn how to adjust.

If the lanes are dry, your ball will "dig in" more when it hooks. In other words, more of the sideways spin of the ball will be translated into hooking power.

If you are right-handed, your ball will hook too far to the left. If you are left-handed, your ball will hook too far to the right.

If the lanes are oily, however, your ball will skid and slide more, and there will be little (if any) hook. This is because the ball cannot get the traction to hook.

If you are right-handed, your ball will miss to the right. If you are left-handed, your ball will miss to the left.

If there is a medium amount of dressing on the lane, no adjustments should be necessary. Just play your regular game.

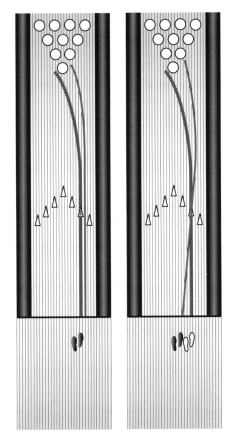

DIALING-IN TO LANE CONDITIONS

Adjusting to lane conditions often is referred to as getting "dialed-in." In competition, the game often goes to the person who recognizes what's happening out on the lane and gets dialed-in first.

There are two basic guidelines for dialing-in to lane conditions:

1. Move in the Direction of the Error.

2. Go With the Flow.

MOVE IN DIRECTION OF ERROR

If your ball consistently misses to the right, move your beginning position to the right on the approach. If your ball misses to the left, move to the left on the approach.

How far should you move? That depends upon how far your shots are off. If you are missing seven boards to the left, move over seven boards, then make fine adjustments from there to get dialed-in precisely.

Aim for the same target out on the lane. Just move to the right or left in the stance. This means that you will be opening or closing your shoulders in relation to the lane.

For right-handed bowlers, your shoulders will open as you move to the left on the approach, and your shoulders will close as you move to the right on the approach.

For left-handed bowlers, your shoulders will open as you move to the right on the approach, and your shoulders will close as you move to the left on the approach.

GO WITH THE FLOW

Going with the flow means taking full advantage of whatever lane condition is present.

This means play a straighter game when the lanes are oily or play a hook game when the lanes are dry.

When the lane conditions are dry, you are going to have a great hook. So take full advantage of this and use the Suitcase Release.

When the lane conditions are very oily, a hook ball is nearly impossible. Also, the sideways spin on the ball will make the ball skid more, meaning you will lose the turn on the ball. So slow down and lay the ball down in front of the foul line. (The ball will not set off the foul light because it passes too quickly.) This will encourage more roll on the ball.

The simplest and most reliable way for a right-hander to strike is to roll the ball into the 1-3 pocket; the 1-2 pocket for left-handers. The ball should hook, allowing it to come in at the proper angle to reduce deflection, thus enabling the ball to continue rolling left to carry the 5 pin.

For a perfect strike, experts agree the ball must hit the 1, 3, 5 and 9 pins (1, 2, 5, 8 for left-handers). One reason for the choice of a hook ball by bowlers is to reduce the chance of deflection. Because speed demands more accuracy, the beginning bowler is urged to work on fundamentals of delivery and let speed be natural.

(A) Bowler should find the point of origin, then line up the ball with the right shoulder and the second arrow, walk straight toward the target and roll the ball toward the target area.

(B) Ball rolls into the 1-3 pocket area (1-2 for left-handers).

(C) Ball drives through the pocket, hitting the 1 and 3 pins (or 1 and 2 pins). The 1 pin knocks down the 2 pin (or 3), starting a chain reaction.

(D) Ball drives through the 5 pin and will soon hit the 9 pin (5 and 8 for left-handers).

(E) Ball has hit the 1, 3, 5 and 9 pins (1, 2, 5, 8 for left-handers), creating the necessary pin action to topple the other six pins.

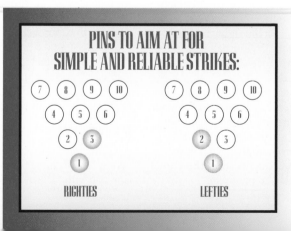

PINS TO AIM AT FOR SIMPLE AND RELIABLE STRIKES:

RIGHTIES | LEFTIES

(F) All 10 pins are knocked down for a strike.

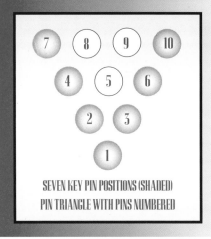

SEVEN KEY PIN POSITIONS (SHADED)
PIN TRIANGLE WITH PINS NUMBERED

MAKING SPARES: EASY AS 1-2-3

Making spares is the way to increase your score faster than anything else. Every time it's your turn to bowl you have two chances to knock down all the pins. These two chances are referred to as a frame. If you knock down all the pins the first time, you get a strike and you don't have to bowl your second shot.

If you don't knock down all the pins the first time, you get a second chance. This is called a spare. If you don't make a spare, it's called an open frame.

The quickest way for a new bowler to get up to a 170 average score or higher is to make all the spares. In bowling, when you make a spare, this is called a spare conversion.

The art of making spares is often called math bowling. Although the term may seem imposing, the only math you really need to know is addition and subtraction.

Making a spare is as simple as 1-2-3.

1. Determine which key pin to hit to make the spare (see diagram above).

2. Line up your feet in the proper position.

3. Aim for the correct target.

Note: To make this easier to understand, there are separate sections for right-handed and left-handed bowlers. After reading the Pin Numbering Section, please refer to either The 1-2-3's of Making Spares: Right-Hand Bowler or The 1-2-3's of Making Spares: Left-Hand Bowler.

LANE BASICS

The first thing to know about a bowling lane is that all lanes are created equal. Every lane in the world is the same width and the same length. The boards are spaced the same distance apart

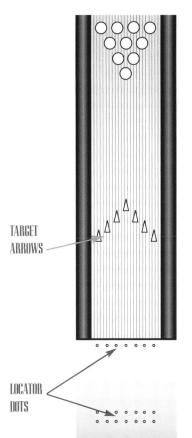

TARGET ARROWS

LOCATOR DOTS

(about one inch). And the locator dots and target arrows are always in the same place. The second thing to know is that the locator dots, target arrows and key outside pins of the pin triangle all line up.

LOCATOR DOTS

There are three sets of locator dots before the foul line. Each dot is spaced five boards from the next. All three sets of locator dots line up with each other.

Note: There also is a set of locator dots beyond the foul line. These dots do not line up with the three sets before the foul line. The dots after the foul line are used by advanced bowlers as "rear gun sights" to fine-tune the angle precisely.

TARGET ARROWS

There are seven target arrows 15 feet out on the lane.

The arrows on the right side are for right-handed bowlers, and the arrows on the left side are for left-handed bowlers.

The target arrows are numbered right-to-left for right-handed bowlers and numbered left-to-right for left-handed bowlers.

We are mainly concerned with the second and third target arrows. You aim at one of these arrows (or sometimes the space between them) when making spares.

Notice the target arrows are in line with the locator dots. The center locator dot corresponds to the center target arrow and so on.

RELATIONSHIP TO PINS

The target lines are also lined up with the key outside pins. By outside pins, we mean the seven pins forming the "V" that is pointed toward you. We also refer to these seven pins as the key

pin positions. *Remember:* any spare can be made by simply aiming at one of the seven key pin positions.

Why are these called target arrows? Because the target arrows are what you aim for! The target arrows mirror the location of the key pin positions. It's much easier to aim for a target that is 15 feet instead of 60 feet away.

In summary, the following are all in line with each other: the three sets of locator dots; the target arrows; the key pin positions.

PIN NUMBERING SYSTEM

There are 10 pins in the pin triangle. To remember the pin numbers, simply start with the head pin as No. 1, then count from left to right.

Note: If you are a left-handed bowler, please skip the following section and read The 1-2-3's of Making Spares: Left-Hand Bowler.

THE 1-2-3s OF MAKING SPARES: RIGHT-HAND BOWLER

Step One: Determine the key pin position

There are literally hundreds of possible spare combinations you might be faced with. Does this mean you have to memorize hundreds of different shots? It's actually much simpler because every shot is a one pin shot!

Remember: any spare can be made by aiming for the proper key pin position. A few examples should help clear this up.

Example One

A common spare is the 4-7. To make this shot, you would aim for the 4 pin. The ball will strike the 4 pin which will knock into the 7 pin. It's a domino effect.

This sample demonstrates a good rule of thumb: the key pin

you want to aim for is usually the pin closest to you.

Example Two

Sometimes, no key pins are left standing. When this is the case, you want to do a make-believe shot. In other words you would aim for where the key position pin was standing. Let's say on your first shot you knocked down all the pins but the 5. What key position would you aim for? The 1 pin. Actually, you would aim the same as you would for a strike.

Example Three

Another common spare is the 3-10 split, also called the baby split. (When one or more pins are left standing, and there is a gap between them, the spare is called a split.)

In this example, you would not aim for either the 3 or the 10. If you did hit one, the other would still be standing. Instead, you would want to aim between them, or where the 6 pin had been standing.

Step Two: Align Your Feet

The next step is to move to either right or left of where you line up for a strike shot. For shots to the right of the head pin, move left; for shots to the left of the head pin, move right.

Note: When making the 1 and/or 5 pin, stay in your strike position without moving right or left.

SHOTS RIGHT OF HEAD PIN

For shots to the right of the head pin, move your stance position left four boards at a time.

In other words: for 3 pin spares, move left four boards

EXAMPLE ONE

EXAMPLE TWO

EXAMPLE THREE

from where you line up for a strike. For 6-pin spares, move left eight boards. For 10-pin spares move left 12 boards.

SHOTS LEFT OF HEAD PIN

For shots to the left of the head pin, move your stance position right in three board

RIGHT OF HEAD PIN

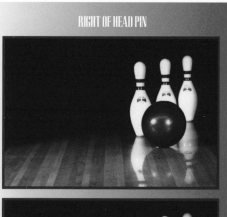

LEFT OF HEAD PIN

increments. In other words: for 2-pin spares, move right three boards from where you line up for a strike. For 4-pin spares, move right six boards. For 7-pin spares move right nine boards.

Note: You may wonder why you move four boards at a time for shots to the right, and three boards at a time for shots to the left. This is because you are throwing against the rotation of the ball when you make spares to the right and with the rotation of the ball when you make spares to the left.

Step Three: Align Your Target

While you should aim for the second arrow on a strike shot, this changes when you are making spares. As you shift over in the stance to make the spare, the target arrow you aim for will also change. Sometimes, you will be aiming between the target arrows.

For 1- and 5-pin spares, do not change your target. Use the second target arrow as you would for a strike.

For all spares to the left of the head pin, aim between the second and third target arrows. For 3-pin spares, also aim between the second and third target arrows. For 6- and 10-pin spares, aim at the third target arrow.

SHOULDER ALIGNMENT WHEN MAKING SPARES

As your position in the stance and your target changes, so will the angle of your body in relation to the lane.

Earlier it was discussed how shoulders could be either opened, closed or straight in relation to the lane. For strike shots, your shoulders should be straight in relation to the lane. When making spares, you should always point your body in the direction of the target. This is called presetting the angle of the shoulders. Remember these three rules:

1. When making 1- and 5-pin spares, keep your shoulders straight in relation to the lane, just as you would when making a strike.

2. When making shots to the right of the head pin, open your shoulders in relation to the lane.

3. When making shots to the left of the head pin, close your shoulders in relation to the lane.

Doing this is easy if you once again imagine that three-foot arrow poised on your right shoulder. Simply point that arrow on your right shoulder at the target and your angle will automatically be correct.

Note: Some new bowlers change their arm swing out or in when aiming at an angle to the lane. Never change your arm swing. Instead, change the angle of your shoulders.

WALK STRAIGHT TO FOUL LINE

Even though your shoulders may be angled open or closed toward the lane, remember this very important point: always walk straight toward the foul line. This means you should never drift right or left or walk at an angle in relation to the lane.

If your shoulders are open or closed, you want to walk slightly on the sides of your feet so that you end up with your feet on the same boards they were on in the stance.

Note: drifting to the right is particularly a problem with the 10-pin shot. This is because your

angle in relation to the lane is sharp, and it is difficult to walk straight to the foul line.

If you have a problem making the 10 pin, check your feet in the stance and at the foul line. Make sure you drift no more than one or two boards.

THE 1-2-3s OF MAKING SPARES: LEFT-HAND BOWLER
Step One: Determine the key pin position

There are literally hundreds of possible spare combinations you might be faced with. Does this mean you have to memorize hundreds of different shots? It's actually much simpler because every shot is a one pin shot!

Remember: Any spare can be made by aiming for the proper key pin position. A few examples should help clear this up.

Example One

A common spare is the 6-10. To make this shot, you would aim for the 6 pin. The ball will strike the 6 pin which will knock into the 10 pin. It's a domino effect. This demonstrates a good rule of thumb: the key pin you want to aim for is usually the pin closest to you.

Example Two

Sometimes, no key pins are left standing. When this is the case, you want to do a make-believe shot. In other words you would aim for where the key position pin was standing.

Let's say on your first shot you knocked down all the pins but the 5. What key position would you aim for? The 1 pin. Actually, you would aim the same as you would for a strike.

Example Three

Another common spare is the 2-7 split, also called the baby split.

EXAMPLE ONE

EXAMPLE TWO

EXAMPLE THREE

either left or right of where you line up for a strike shot. For shots to the left of the head pin, move right; for shots to the right of the head pin, move left.

Note: When making the 1 and/or 5 pin, stay in your strike position without moving left or right.

SHOTS LEFT OF HEAD PIN

For shots to the left of the head pin, move your stance position right four boards at a time. In other words: For 2-pin spares, move right four boards from where you line up for a strike. For 4-pin spares, move right eight boards. For 7-pin spares move right 12 boards.

SHOTS RIGHT OF HEAD PIN

For shots to the right of the head pin, move your stance position left in three board increments. In other words: for 3-pin spares, move left three boards from where you line up for a strike. For 6-pin spares, move left six boards. For 10-pin spares move left nine boards.

Note: You may wonder why you move four boards at a time for shots to the left, and three boards at a time for shots to the right. This is because you are throwing against the rotation of the ball when you make spares to the left and with the rotation of the ball when you make spares to the right.

Step Three: Align Your Target

Making a strike shot you should aim for the second arrow was mentioned earlier. This changes when you are making spares. As you shift over in the stance to make the spare, the

(When one or more pins are left standing, and there is a gap between them, the spare is called a split.)

In this example, you would not aim for either the 2 or the 7. If you did hit one, the other would still be standing. Instead, you would want to aim between them, or where the 4 pin had been standing.

Step Two: Align Your Feet

The next step is to move to

target arrow you aim for will also change. Sometimes, you will be aiming between the target arrows.

For 1- and 5-pin spares, do not change your target. Use the second target arrow as you would for a strike. For all spares to the right of the head pin, aim between the second and third target arrows. For 2-pin spares, also aim between the second and third target arrows. For 4- and 7-pin spares, aim at the third target arrow.

SHOULDER ALIGNMENT WHEN MAKING SPARES

As your position in the stance and your target changes, so will the angle of your body in relation to the lane. Earlier it was mentioned how shoulders could be either opened, closed or straight in relation to the lane. For strike shots, your shoulders should be straight in relation to the lane. When making spares, this is not always true. What is true is that you should always point your body in the direction of the target.

This is called presetting the angle of the shoulders.

Remember these three rules:

1. When making 1 and 5 pin position spares, keep your shoulders straight in relation to the lane, just as you would when making a strike.

2. When making shots to the left of the head pin, open your shoulders in relation to the lane.

3. When making shots to the right of the head pin, close your shoulders in relation to the lane.

Doing this is easy if you once again imagine that three foot

HOW TO SPARE

lefties

arrow poised on your left shoulder. Simply point that arrow on your left shoulder at the target and your angle will automatically be correct.

Note: Some new bowlers change their arm swing out or in when aiming at an angle to the lane. Never change your arm swing. Instead, change the angle of your shoulders.

WALK STRAIGHT TO FOUL LINE

Even though your shoulders may be angled open or closed toward the lane, remember this very important point: always walk straight toward the foul line.

This means you should never drift left or right or walk at an angle in relation to the lane. If your shoulders are open or closed, you want to walk slightly on the sides of your feet so that you end up with your feet on the same boards they were on in the stance.

Note: Drifting to the right is particularly a problem with the 7-pin shot. This is because your angle in relation to the lane is sharp, and it is difficult to walk straight to the foul line.

If you have a problem making the 7 pin, check your feet in the stance and at the foul line. Make sure you drift no more than one or two boards.

lefties

LEAGUES AND TOURNAMENTS

You should now be ready for perhaps the most exciting part of bowling – competing in leagues and tournaments. The ABC, WIBC and YABA coordinate league activities at thousands of bowling centers in the United States. Leagues organized by these national associations are called "sanctioned leagues."

In addition to sanctioned league competition, there is sanctioned tournament competition. These tournaments are organized at the local, state and national level. There are different tournaments for different classes of bowlers, so even beginning bowlers can enjoy the thrill of one-on-one competition in a tournament.

Because of the handicap system used by leagues, new bowlers can compete successfully in any sanctioned league. The handicap system provides newer

bowlers with lower averages a "head start" by giving them handicap points before the game even starts.

There are also tournaments that give newer bowlers handicap points so they can compete one-on-one with bowlers whose averages are far higher.

To join a league, all you have to do is call your local bowling center. Someone at the control counter will be happy to assist you. Fall/Winter leagues usually start around Labor Day and last 12-36 weeks. Summer leagues run from May to August.

Almost all the meticulous work is handled by the league secretary. The league secretary keeps all of your personal and team records, figures out your averages and handicaps each week, schedules the teams you will play and what lanes you will use, and posts team and individual standings.

All of this information will be posted on the bulletin board at the bowling center.

All you have to do is apply for ABC, WIBC, or YABA membership, show up each week, check the bulletin board, bowl the best you can and pay your league dues.

Make sure you are matched with people whose company you enjoy. Ask someone at the control desk or even the bowling proprietor personally what league would be the best for you.

After all, the bowling proprietor really has one goal: to make sure you enjoy yourself and keep coming back.

For single people there are mixed leagues; for couples there are couples leagues; and, there are numerous men's, women's and youth leagues. There are also many special interest leagues. These include senior citizens, career/vocational, PTA and local school leagues.

The nice part about special interest leagues is that you know you will be in the company of those who share common interests with you. Also make sure you are matched with bowlers whose abilities are close to yours.

Most bowling centers have one or more league(s) comprised of top notch bowlers. Even though the extra handicap points will help you out, you probably won't enjoy bowling a 120 game when all around you are bowling 180 or better. Ask around the bowling center and find out which leagues are for newer players.

Also, make sure you get along well with your team members. Nothing can ruin the fun of bowling more than conflict between teammates. The safest bet is to talk some of your friends into joining with you, then start your own team.

Above all, don't feel self-conscious about having a low average at first. The lower your average, the more handicap points you will get as a head start. Also, as a new player you will improve much faster than seasoned teammates. These two factors will make you a real asset to your team.

THE HANDICAP SYSTEM

As we mentioned, league competition is based on a handicap system. The handicap system spots bowlers with lower averages extra points. It's like getting a head start before the game even begins.

You really don't need to understand that much about handicaps because your league secretary will calculate your new average and handicap every week you bowl. It is helpful, though, to understand what is going on behind the scenes.

When you bowl on a league your average is calculated by the league secretary each week. Your average is a running total of all your scores divided by the number of games you have bowled that season. This means that if you start bowling better each week, your average will go up.

A handicap is based on a percentage of the difference between your team average and the average of the other team. This percentage is usually between 70% and 100%. (In the following example, we will use the 90% handicap system.)

A team can have anywhere from 1-5 players on it. In this example, let's assume that you have five players on your team.

Your Team
Player 1 Average = 140
Player 2 Average = 135
Player 3 Average = 120
Player 4 Average = 115
Player 5 Average = 130
Total Team Average = 640

TEAM USA, the official bowling team representing the United States, happens to be in town and wants to play your team in their first exhibition game! This is their current team average:

TEAM USA
Player 1 Average = 225
Player 2 Average = 210
Player 3 Average = 215
Player 4 Average = 220
Player 5 Average = 210
Total Team Average = 1,080

The difference between the two team averages is 440 points (1,080-640=440).

Assuming that you are playing with the 90% handicap system, you would multiply the difference by 90% to determine your handicap: (440 X 90%=396).

This means that before you even begin the game you will have a head start of 396 points. The starting score will be Your Team: 396 points; TEAM USA: 0.

HANDICAP, SCRATCH AND BRACKET TOURNAMENTS
Sanctioned ABC/WIBC tournaments are a great way to enjoy the thrill of one-on-one competition. There are three basic types of tournaments:

•**Handicap Tournaments:** in a handicap tournament, you will receive a handicap based on the difference between your bowling average and the field of participants in the tournament.

Suppose you have an average of 150 and the person you are bowling against has an average of 190. The difference is 40 pins. If this is a 90% handicap tournament, you will be spotted 36 points before the match even begins!

A handicap tournament is a great opportunity for a new bowler to win. As a new bowler, it's much easier for you to throw a couple extra strikes and bowl 100 pins over your average than it is for a 200 bowler to bowl 100 pins over his or her average!

•**Scratch Tournaments:** in scratch tournaments, there are no handicaps. The final points at the end of the match are all that count.

•**Bracket Tournaments:** in bracket tournaments, you only compete against those whose averages are close to yours. In others words, there will be divisions, such as a 100-115 division, a 115-130 division, and so on.

Some bracket tournaments are closed to only those individuals who have a certain average. For example, there are tournaments only for players whose averages are over 180; conversely, there are tournaments only for players whose averages are under 180.

Remember: there's prize money to be won at a tournament, and you could be the winner! Sometimes even local tournaments offer top prizes in the thousands of dollars. If you compete in state or national tournaments, you also get the opportunity to travel and see new places.

Bowling is a singular sport. Even in league competition, when a person gets up to bowl it's only the bowler versus the pins. Perhaps this is why the mental elements of sports and competition play such an important role in bowling.

There are many different aspects when talking about bowling's mental game. For example, some people become depressed if they don't see dramatic improvement all at once. As with many other areas in life, progress in bowling happens in stages, with long plateaus in between.

Other people try so hard to remember everything they need to do they "over-think" the game. Often, bowlers become too excited or "psyched-out" before a big game. Conversely, others lack motivation, enthusiasm and energy for a variety of reasons.

After the physical skills of bowling have been acquired, mastering the mind and the mental game is the next step. You need methods to help boost your confidence, avoid over-thinking, develop positive mental images, and become psyched-up instead of psyched-out.

These techniques are useful for more than bowling or even sports in general. They can help you lead a happier life, reduce stress and anxiety, and succeed in any endeavor.

Note: The majority of this material has been provided by the United States Olympic Committee Elite Coaches Workshop in Sports Psychology.

COMPETENCE = CONFIDENCE

People feel good about doing the things they do well. As your skill increases, your mental attitude toward the game will improve as well.

Confidence comes when you know you have what it takes to get the job done. In bowling it comes when you have mastered the basics, know how to adjust to lane conditions and dial into the strike pocket and when adjusting for a difficult spare conversion is a reflex action. Mastering these techniques can only come through practice.

MAKE BOWLING FUN!

The term "practice" conjures up images of an individual performing the same boring task over and over again. This is not the case in bowling. Every time you get up to bowl you are faced with a different set of challenges. The lane conditions will be different than the last time. You will be different. That's the challenge of bowling. And part of the fun!

Don't get so wrapped up in improving your game that you forget to enjoy the sport. It is strongly recommended new bowlers join a league where they can make new friends, improve their game and have a lot of fun at the same time.

POSITIVE SELF TALK

Each of us has a little voice inside that talks to us. What is that voice saying to you? Are you receiving positive or negative reinforcement?

What your inner voice says to you has a great influence on your mental attitude. While it is true you can be your own worst critic, make sure you are giving yourself positive suggestions, not negative criticism.

Make an audio tape for yourself. Record some music on it that makes you feel good. Talk to yourself on this tape. Remind yourself you are improving. Review past achievements that made you feel proud. Fantasize about future improvements and achievements. *Remember:* you are what you think.

POSITIVE MENTAL IMAGERY

Mental imagery is a more intense form of internal communication than self-talk. Think of mental imagery as a vivid daydream.

Most forms of mental imagery are playbacks from our memory. Mental images can seem so real that all the senses are engaged. In very vivid images, the visual, auditory, tactile (touch), olfactory (smells and taste), and kinesthetic (body movement and motion) senses all become involved.

Mental imagery can be so vivid that thousands of minute details are visualized at once. Think about lining up in the stance and making a shot. This can be visualized in one vivid mental image, although it takes thousands of words to describe it in a book.

Everyone experiences mental imagery in some form. Recently, however, researchers have learned to develop mental imagery into a powerful tool for improving skill, generating positive mental attitudes, and increasing one's drive and energy.

There are two types of mental imagery:

Goal-oriented imagery involves developing mental images of success. It can be an image as complex as bowling strike after strike, finally making that 300 game and hearing the roar of the crowd in the background. Or it can be a simple image, such as converting a difficult spare.

Process imagery involves imagining the physical process itself. This is a great way to supplement your actual practice sessions and improve.

WHY IMAGERY WORKS

There are four basic reasons why practicing imagery helps athletes perform better.

1. When you relive a moment or daydream, the brain actually sends signals to the appropriate muscles. These signals are called neuromuscular impulses. They are weaker versions of the same neuromuscular impulses that make your muscles work. When you imagine yourself bowling, you are actually strengthening the neural pathways!

2. Practicing imagery "programs" your mind with a set of instructions so that during an actual game the movements are more familiar and therefore more natural.

3. Imagery helps you maintain your emotional peak. When practicing imagery, you imagine yourself being successful and doing everything perfectly. This helps you achieve a positive mental attitude geared toward success while alleviating feelings of stress and depression.

4. When used just before competition, imagery prepares the mind and body to work while clearing away negative thoughts and distractions. In effect, it replaces worrying with positive mental images, boosting your confidence.

PRACTICING IMAGERY

Imagery is a skill that takes practice to develop. The more you practice mental imagery, the easier it becomes. The mental images also will become more vivid. Here are a few hints to help you practice mental imagery.

• Combine imagery practice with actual practice. They will reinforce each other.

• Practice imagery when you are alone in a quiet place. Outside influences will interfere with your "daydreaming" and weaken the effect. With practice, however, you will find you can practice imagery even in a crowd. This should be your goal.

• Practice imagery in conjunction with self-hypnosis, relaxation or meditation. This will help focus your attention, as well as making the mental images more vivid.

RELAXATION AND BREATHING

The techniques we just described are more effective when combined with various relaxation and breathing techniques. Relaxation techniques help focus your mind on what you are doing.

In addition, relaxation – when practiced just before an actual game – will relieve stress and anxiety, allowing you to bowl your best.

There are many different relaxation techniques. Any of these techniques may be used to put your mind and body in a deep relaxation state. The following method is similar to one that has been successfully used by TEAM USA bowlers and other athletes at the United States Olympic Training Center.

1. Find a quiet place where you can be alone and relaxed for 10 or 15 minutes.

2. Lie on your back. Place your hands by your side. Keep your legs straight, not crossed. As soon as you are comfortable, close your eyes.

3. Begin breathing deeply and slowly. Make sure to use your diaphragm when you breathe. You'll know that you are breathing deeply with your diaphragm when your stomach – not your chest – begins to rise and fall slowly. Take a deep breath, hold it in for a few seconds, then slowly let it out. It may be helpful to breathe in with your nose and out with your mouth. After a minute or two, you will notice both mind and body are moving toward a more relaxed state.

4. Try to visualize with your mind one of your feet. When you can "see with your mind," concentrate on relaxing all of the muscles in the foot.

For example, you may say to yourself, "My foot is becoming heavy, heavy with relaxation. I can feel all the muscles loosening and relaxing." Don't try to concentrate too hard, or you will "over-think" and actually generate the anxiety you are trying to relieve. Let it happen naturally. Remember that these techniques take practice in order to fully master them.

If you feel any anxiety, stop, concentrate on your breathing and let your mind naturally drop back into a relaxed state.

5. Relax the muscles of the other foot in the same way, then one leg, then the other leg. Continue slowly up the body until you are totally relaxed and in an even deeper mental state.

6. In this deeply relaxed state, your mind will be much more receptive to suggestion than during normal consciousness. This is the best time to practice Self-Talk and Mental Imagery. Remember, you don't have to do it for long. A few minutes a day is sufficient.

7. When finished, concentrate once more on your breathing. Stretch your arms and legs slowly. Then open your eyes.

The use of breathing as a relaxation technique can also be used during a game. The next time you feel stress or anxiety, stop, take a few deep breaths and let your mind clear. You will automatically feel more relaxed.

MENTALLY PREPARING FOR A GAME

Preparing for a game starts before you even get to the bowling center. Obviously proper sleep the night before is one of the best ways to prepare your mind and body to perform at top proficiency. As far as eating, don't be hungry or full, but somewhere in between.

Listen to your self-talk tape on the way to the bowling center, and visualize yourself going out there and playing your best.

When you get to the bowling center, get a feel for the condition of the lane. Start planning how you will adjust to the lane if your first impressions are confirmed.

Before you get up to bowl, imagine a circular area somewhere between the ball return and the scoring table. This will be your think circle where you will wait when you are the next person up to bowl.

When in the think circle, visualize what you will do, from lining up into the stance to ending up in the finish position. Imagine the ball following that "Line in Your Mind."

Then, when it's your turn, align yourself in the stance and do it without hesitation. Once you line up in the stance, the time for thinking is over. Your decisions have already been made in the think circle. If you think in the stance, you may "over-think" and end up psyching yourself out.

Practice the techniques mentioned here and you will soon realize improvement in not only your bowling score but your overall mental attitude as well.

Many first-time bowlers are confused about keeping score. While scoring in bowling may appear difficult, once a few basic points are understood, it's as easy as keeping score in any other sport.

Automatic scorekeepers, now common in many bowling centers, have taken a lot of the work out of keeping score. But it's still important to know a few basic points.

BASICS OF SCORING

In bowling, a game consists of 10 frames. During a frame, you get two chances to knock down all the pins. If you knock down all the pins the first time, you don't take your second shot, but instead go on to the next frame.

When you bowl a frame, three things can happen:

• **Strike:** You knock down all the pins on your first shot of a frame.

• **Spare:** You knock down all the pins in two shots.

• **Open:** There are still pins standing after you take your two shots.

Note: You may have heard the term "split." With a split,

after the first shot, there are pins standing in such a way that it is difficult for you to knock the remainder down in the next shot. In other words, you will have to either aim between the remaining pins or skid one pin into the other(s) in order to knock them down.

Whether a shot is a split or not has nothing to do with the score. If you knock down the remaining pins, you'll have a spare; if you don't, you'll have an open frame.

Scoring in bowling gives you extra "rewards" or bonuses if you knock down all the pins in a frame. If you knock them all down on the first shot of a frame (a strike) you get an opportunity to make more "bonus" points than if it takes two shots (a spare).

Here's how it works:

• An open frame is worth the number of pins you knocked down in the frame.

• A spare is worth 10 points plus your next shot.

• A strike is worth 10 points plus your next two shots.

THE SCORECARD

The lines of a scoreboard are where bowlers keep track

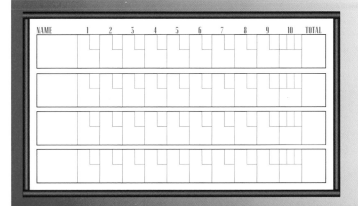

of their individual scores during a game.

Notice there are 10 large squares on every line. These squares represent the 10 frames you bowl in a game. In the right hand corner of each of the first nine frames, there is a smaller square. In the 10th frame, though, notice there are

SYMBOLS USED ON THE SCORECARD

There are four basic symbols used on the scorecard:

• If you make a strike, put a large "X" in the little square. (There's no need to write "10" to the left of the square, because the "X" means that you knocked down all 10 pins on your first try.)

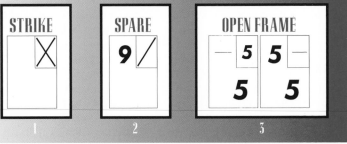

three squares running along the top. This is because the 10th or last frame of a game differs somewhat from the first nine.

For now, let's concentrate on the first nine frames. The diagrams above show sample frames on a scorecard.

Briefly, here's how to score a frame:

Record the pins you knock down on your first shot to the left of the little square.

If you bowl an open frame, record the pins you knock down on your second shot in the little square to the right. This also is where you write the strike (X) and spare (/) symbols.

Keep a running total of the game in the bottom portion of the frame.

For example, suppose on the first shot of the first frame you knock down six pins. On the next shot, you knock down two pins. The first frame would be scored as in the sample above.

Notice that we didn't put any score in the "running total" area in the bottom of the frame. This is because a strike is worth 10 pins plus the next two shots. You can't record the running total for this frame until you have made two more shots.

• If you make a spare, put a slash "/" in the little square. Also, record the pins you knocked down on the first shot to the left of the little square. (There's no need to record your score of the second shot, since the slash mark indicates that you knocked down the remaining pins.)

As with the example of a strike, we have not filled-in the "running total" in Sample 2. This is because a spare is worth 10 points plus the next shot. You can't fill in the running total until you have made one more shot.

• If you miss all the pins during a shot, record a dash "–". If you miss all the pins during

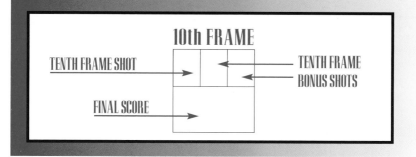

10th FRAME

TENTH FRAME SHOT

FINAL SCORE

TENTH FRAME
BONUS SHOTS

your first shot, put the dash to the left of the little square; if you miss all the pins during the second shot, put the dash inside the little square.

• You may have noticed that sometimes a bowler will circle the number to the right of the little square. This indicates that the bowler was left with a split for the second shot. Use of the circle has nothing to do with actual scoring. It just signifies a difficult spare shot.

THE 10TH FRAME

The 10th frame is different than the other frames. In the 10th frame, you can get up to three shots. That's why there are three small squares in this frame.

The reason the 10th frame is different is because you have to be able to finish out the game. Let's suppose you make a strike in the 10th frame. According to the scoring rules of bowling, a strike is worth 10 points plus the next two shots. But there are no more frames to be played; the 10th frame is the last. That's why you have the opportunity to make up to two extra shots during the 10th frame.

Here are the general rules:
If you make a strike during the 10th frame, you get two extra

shots. If you make a spare during the 10th frame, you get one extra shot. If you open or leave pins standing during the 10th frame, you get no extra shots. A few examples should help clarify this.

Example One

Suppose that you begin the 10th frame with a score of 150. On your first shot, you get a strike. This means you get two more chances. On your next shot, you get a nine, and you miss the remaining pin on your final shot. The final two frames would look like this:

Notice that adding up your shots on the final 10th frame is simple. You just add them all up!

Example Two

In this example, your score in the ninth frame is 160. On your first shot in the 10th frame, you get nine. On your next shot you get the remaining pin, earning a spare. In a normal frame, that would be it, but in the 10th frame, you get another shot. On this shot, you get nine. Your total in the 10th frame is 19, which added to 160 gives you a final score of 179.

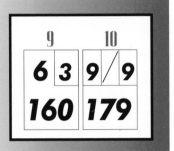

Note: Notice in this example there is still one pin left standing at the end of the game. In this case, before another person can bowl you will have to use the reset button on the return to set up the pins for the next player.

Example Three

This time you enter the 10th frame with a score of 165. On your first shot you get eight. On your next shot, you get one, leaving a pin. This means you have an open frame in the 10th. There is no extra shot. Your score for the 10th frame is nine, giving you a final score of 174.

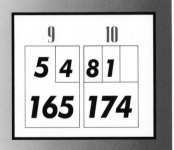

SCORING A SAMPLE GAME

This sample game will demonstrate everything we have discussed previously. If you can follow the steps frame-by-frame, you will have no difficulty scoring your own game.

In the first frame, you bowl a spare. Notice we have not filled in a score for the frame, because you have to bowl another shot first. In the second frame, you bowl a strike. The 10 from this shot is added to the 10 from the first frame to give you a score of 20 in the first frame. We have not filled in a score for the second frame, because you have to bowl the next two shots first.

In the third frame, you make eight on your first shot, then miss the remaining pins on your second shot. We can now fill in the second frame $(20+10+8=38)$ and the third frame $(38+8=46)$.

Since you're beginning to warm up, you bowl strikes in the fourth and fifth Frames. Indicate strikes for these frames but don't fill in the scores yet since a strike is worth 10 points plus the next two shots.

In the sixth frame, you bowl a nine on the first shot, then pick up the remaining pin for a spare. Now we can fill in the running totals for frame four $(46+10+10+9=75)$ and frame five $(75+10+9+1=95)$.

In the seventh frame, you knock down nine pins on your first shot, then miss the last pin on the second shot. We can now fill in the running totals for frame six $(95+10+9=114)$ and frame seven $(114+9=123)$.

In the eighth and ninth frames, you bowl strikes. Indicate these strikes but don't fill in any running

	1	2	3	4	5	6	7	8	9	10
FIRST FRAME	/									

	1	2	3	4	5	6	7	8	9	10
SECOND FRAME	6 /	X								
	20									

	1	2	3	4	5	6	7	8	9	10
THIRD FRAME	6 /	X	8 –							
	20	**38**	**46**							

	1	2	3	4	5	6	7	8	9	10
FOURTH FRAME	6 /	X	8 –	X						
	20	**38**	**46**							

	1	2	3	4	5	6	7	8	9	10
FIFTH FRAME	6 /	X	8 –	X	X					
	20	**38**	**46**							

	1	2	3	4	5	6	7	8	9	10
SIXTH FRAME	6 /	X	8 –	X	X	9 /				
	20	**38**	**46**	**75**	**95**					

	1	2	3	4	5	6	7	8	9	10
SEVENTH FRAME	6 /	X	8 –	X	X	9 /	9 –			
	20	**38**	**46**	**75**	**95**	**114**	**123**			

	1	2	3	4	5	6	7	8	9	10
EIGHTH FRAME	6 /	X	8 –	X	X	9 /	9 –	X		
	20	**38**	**46**	**75**	**95**	**114**	**123**			

	1	2	3	4	5	6	7	8	9	10
NINTH FRAME	6 /	X	8 –	X	X	9 /	9 –	X	X	
	20	**38**	**46**	**75**	**95**	**114**	**123**			

	1	2	3	4	5	6	7	8	9	10
TENTH FRAME	6 /	X	8 –	X	X	9 /	9 –	X	X	9 / X
	20	**38**	**46**	**75**	**95**	**114**	**123**	**152**	**172**	**192**

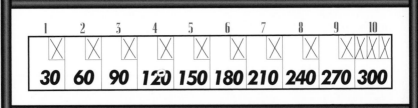

1	2	3	4	5	6	7	8	9	10
X	X	X	X	X	X	X	X	X	XXX
30	60	90	120	150	180	210	240	270	300

totals, since we can't yet. In the first shot of the 10th frame, you knock down nine pins. Now we can fill in running total for the eighth frame (123+10+10+9=152). On your next shot, you knock down the remaining pin and make the spare. Now we can fill in the running total for the ninth frame (152+10+9+1=172).

Since it is the 10th frame and you have made a spare, you take your extra shot and make a strike. Now you can add up the three shots of the 10th frame and get your final game score (172+9+1+10=192).

300: THE PERFECT GAME

The highest score you can get in bowling is 300. To attain a 300 game, you must bowl 12 consecutive strikes, the most possible in one game. That is why a 300 also is known as a "perfect" game.

INSTRUCTIONAL CONCLUSION

Now that you know the basics of bowling, the next step if you haven't already done so, is to find a league that fits your needs and schedule.

Check the nearest bowling center for times and dates available in your area. Or ask your friends to see if they already bowl in a league.

If you want to learn more about the sport, you should work with a USA Bowling Certified Coach. He or she can get you started on special clinics and manuals that cover more advanced features while providing you with the individual instruction you truly need to improve your game.

For more information, contact **USA Bowling at 414/421-9008.**

We wish you the best of luck in your bowling career, whether it becomes a once-a-week diversion or your full-time profession. Remember: once you know what to do, all that remains is to practice until the techniques are yours. And you will improve. Bowling has always attracted positive people who have what it takes to succeed.

INSTRUCTIONAL CONCLUSION

QUESTION

What are the odds of rolling a 300 game?

ANSWER

There is no scientific way to determine this. The unscientific method, however, involves the number of games bowled and number of sanctioned 300 earned in a bowling season. It is estimated league bowlers roll an average of 100 games per season (90 league, 10 tournament). With about four million sanctioned league bowlers rolling about 400 million games and more than 35,000 perfect games rolled each year, the odds are about one 300 for approximately every 11,500 games. Since women and youth roll far fewer 300s than men, their odds are much greater.

QUESTION

What is the origin of the term "Dutch 200"?

ANSWER

The Dutch 200 refers to a game in which strikes and spares are alternated. The term is believed to be a take-off of "Dutch treat" where two people share the cost of a date. Strikes and spares share the game in alternate frames in a "Dutch treat 200" manner which with usage was reduced to "Dutch 200."

QUESTION

What is the origin of the term "Brooklyn strike"?

ANSWER

This refers to shots that "cross over" the 1-3 pocket for right-handers and 1-2 for left-handers and produces a strike. It originated in New York where people would "cross over" to Brooklyn from Manhattan. A side term "Jersey side" references left-handers and refers to people crossing over from Manhattan to New Jersey.

QUESTION

What is the origin of the term "Turkey"?

ANSWER

The term dates back to before the turn of the 20th century. In those years, scoring was much more difficult and to get three strikes in a row was quite an achievement. During Thanksgiving or Christmas week, the proprietor would present a live turkey to the first person on each team who scored three consecutive strikes. The term has carried over ever since.

QUESTION

What is the bowling capital of the United States?

ANSWER

This depends on the criteria used. If it is for sheer number of bowlers, Detroit is the hands-down winner. If it's because Bowling Headquarters has long been located there, it's Milwaukee. If it's because of the International Bowling Museum and Hall of Fame, St. Louis wins. Or if it's best access to bowling, it's Appleton-Oshkosh-Neenah, Wis., which according to the Places Rated Almanac has 522 residents per lane.

"You're never too old to bowl" is a familiar phrase and with the growing number of senior leagues throughout the country, it couldn't be more true. Age is not a detriment to being able to bowl, particularly if you can adjust your game to what's happening to your body.

The older a person becomes the more difficult some things are to achieve. Fortunately, bowling is a recreation that can be taken up and enjoyed even at 65 or 70 years of age. It's not essential that you bowled as a youngster, or even bowled at all, although it would be an asset. Bowling is a game that can be learned at any age, and there are right ways and wrong ways to proceed.

First, understand matching professionals in the scoring column is out of the question. Instead of 200 games, most senior bowlers should settle for an occasional 160 or 170. Being able to bowl regularly provides the major source of enjoyment for seniors, not pursuit of high scores.

High average performers who are reaching senior age status might continue to be proficient. And most likely, they're still competing in good leagues with high average players. But for most people, age can be a bitter pill because of individual pride. If you can understand the situation – know that everyone tends to lose a little something no matter what the endeavor – bowling can be a good part of your life.

That's the mental aspect of the game which could keep a one-time top performer from enjoying bowling in senior leagues.

A newcomer doesn't face that situation, and expectations aren't nearly so high.

Physical ailments or handicaps can be overcome. A bowler still can enjoy the sport. While fundamentals, such as a deep knee bend, might be difficult to do, there are adjustments which can help the bowler.

INFORMATION TO HELP SENIOR BOWLERS

• Choose a ball that is not too heavy. Some older bowlers, those in their 80s and 90s, should use eight, nine or 10 pound balls. Since high scoring is difficult, enjoyment and satisfaction of getting an extra strike or two and making spares is most important. A good way to check whether the ball is too heavy is to keep track of your scores. If there is a consistent pattern of good scoring early then lower scoring in the final frames, the ball probably is too heavy and is starting to control the bowler rather than the bowler controlling the ball. Then it's time for lighter equipment.

• Consider increasing the grip to three or four fingers. If arthritis, rheumatism or any other physical ailment is making it difficult to hold the ball, additional finger holes will make the ball easier to hold and swing. The lifting effect won't be better, but the advantage of better control at point of release will be benefit enough.

• For those who have not bowled before, a one or two step approach is best to teach the pendulum swing and release of the ball. Most senior newcomers cannot coordinate swing and steps. Generally three or four steps will be taken before the ball is moved. If the bowler does push the ball away on the first step, normally the feet do not move forward fast enough and the ball already is swinging and ready to leave the hand after only one or two steps. Concentrate on a one or two step approach to learn the basics of release.

• Once the swing and release are learned, try to incorporate the basic four-step approach. But if the four-step is too difficult, don't hesitate to go back to the two-step approach. After all, the right-hander's main concern is to be able to roll the ball toward the 1-3 pocket and knock down as many pins as possible. If you can accomplish this with a two-step or one-step approach, why not do it? Remember, the main concern is the enjoyment of being able to participate. The new bowler should learn to roll the ball toward the 1-3 pocket (1-2 for lefthanders). A new bowler should study the basics explained in this book. If you are physically capable, everything written about grip, etc. in this book applies to you.

• In nearly every case, a senior bowler should use a conventional grip. There is less demand on the hand with the conventional, and it is easier to control. You give up something when switching to a fingertip, but in the long run you'll find more enjoyment and fewer problems as you continue to bowl.

The lack of mobility in bending at the foul line during release is common among senior bowlers. Concentration is essential to overcome the lack of knee bend.

Or try bending more at the waist. Keep the arm straight and swing it toward the target. There is a natural tendency to pull the ball and turn the body when the knees aren't bent. Concentrate on a straight arm swing.

•Adjustments to lane conditions by seniors are essential because most bowlers roll the ball slowly, which allows more time for the natural tendency of the lane to take the ball away from the strike pocket. No matter how or where the bowler stands, adjust by turning the bowling shoulder to compensate for the previous shot.

If you are standing on the approach in a position so the shoulder is lined up with the 3-pin, walk straight, swing straight and the ball goes too far to the left, the next time the bowling shoulder should be turned more to the right. Rather than looking for specific arrows or boards on the lane, simplify your adjustment. Keep the ball in the general area around the headpin all the time.

Because rhythm and coordination may not be what they used to be, staying in the headpin area is best for good first ball results and easier spare shots. By pointing the bowling shoulder more to the right or left, depending on where the previous shot wound up, this simple adjustment can help the senior bowler become more accurate, particularly shooting spares.

•Think about the adjustment without worrying about hitting specific spots on the lane. Start your approach somewhere near the center and roll the ball in the vicinity of the second arrow. Then make shoulder adjustments

until you're pretty well zeroed in on the headpin. Once you've found your starting point and can walk fairly straight and release the ball fairly straight, spare shooting will become much easier by using a simple shoulder adjustment. Of course, many seniors become adept at the scientific spare system mentioned earlier so don't hesitate to try it.

•What kind of ball roll is best for seniors? Straight ball? Hook ball? Backup ball? Most seniors have very little lift at point of release. And most roll a straight ball. If a senior can control a hook, that's the best ball to roll. But a straight ball is easier to control and usually the bowler is more accurate.

Unless a bowler has been a backup ball practitioner, it's unlikely seniors will roll backups. Most will roll it straight. However, due to lane conditions, a straight ball might not always go straight. In fact, with lack of speed, the ball often will roll off to the right or left, even if it starts out straight down the middle. Learning the best adjustment is one answer for hitting the headpin, but having equipment which will best help your game can be invaluable.

•Many senior bowlers have their own bowling ball, bag and shoes. Although house equipment is available, bowlers who have their own have an edge. Often selecting a house ball is done with little concern or thought. Your selection might not be the best for you. By purchasing your own ball and having it properly fitted, the pro shop professional can provide a great assistance to your game.

If you can describe how your ball reacts on the lanes to the person fitting you, chances are a shift in weight within the ball to one side or the other can eliminate your problem of the ball rolling away from the headpin.

What about the good bowler who still possesses outstanding ability, but is getting older? The older a bowler becomes, past a certain point, of course, the weight of the bowling ball should be lightened. Go down a half-pound or pound, but keep the same type of grip if you can handle it. You might sacrifice a little on a pocket hit or two, but if accuracy improves and you still control the ball, that should make up the difference. If your scores tend to drop in the last game, your hand could be tiring. Try a little less weight.

All of the basics taught in this book won't apply to senior bowlers. With age comes lack of stamina and strength, but not to the point where you can't enjoy bowling! Often a senior bowler has trouble rolling strikes. Everyone agrees rolling the ball into the 1-3 pocket is the best idea. Yet there are seniors who have more action on the ball when they hit the Brooklyn (1-2) side. Since senior bowlers should be seeking enjoyment and companionship from the game, following the rules doesn't always apply.

A light ball going into the 1-3 pocket leaves the 5 pin or 5-8 spare combination most of the time. The reason is there isn't enough hook and not enough speed and the ball deflects away from the 1-3 pocket. If your game could stand a few more strikes, try rolling for the crossover strike. Sometimes the ball deflects so hard that the pins have a greater tendency to mix.

Remember. You are an individual and what is good for someone else might not be good for you. There are certain things you have to do that younger bowlers do not. Remember enjoyment of the game, being able to look forward to the once or twice a week activity, is the most important aspect. If it takes a lighter ball or a different grip than you used when you were 30, make the change. Don't let physical ailments deter your enthusiasm. Go out and bowl the way it is most fun for you!

A good place to begin any teaching program or instructional course for youth bowlers is with the approach. And the best advice is "slow down."

Young bowlers have strength and stamina and an overpowering desire to knock down all 10 pins on the first shot. Convincing the stars of tomorrow to learn the four-step approach and let the ball roll easily into the strike area can be quite a task. But for every bowler who is taught the right way at a young age, the lesson will last a lifetime.

There are so many outstanding instructional programs for young bowlers today, particularly the USA Junior Olympic Coaching Program. Anyone who is interested in the sport should be able to learn the basics. Improvement, of course, depends on ability, desire and a willingness to practice.

WHERE TO START

If the bowlers are strong enough to handle a bowling ball, they should learn the four-step approach first. It is imperative

the bowler understand the importance of coordinating the rhythm of the pendulum swing with the four steps of the approach and the straight follow through. **Emphasis must be placed on the first and second steps. That's where the youth can slow down so the ball and final step arrive at the foul line at the same time.** If the bowler understands a smooth delivery and rolling ball are the most effective ways to improve scoring, and a hard thrower often loses strikes because the ball moves through the pins so quickly they do not have an opportunity to mix well, they are on the right track toward becoming a good bowler.

With so many people bowling at such young ages, learning the four-step approach can be difficult or impossible, in some cases. A young bowler should begin with good instruction rather than trying to learn the game by trial and error. A youngster sees others bowl and doesn't bother to count the steps. The only thing of importance seems to be to run to the foul line and throw the ball. If a bowler can be taught the right way, eliminating bad habits before they form, good results will come much quicker.

The weight of the ball is extremely important. An 8, 9 or 10-year-old can't handle much more than eight pounds. And often they won't be able to swing the ball, particularly taking a four-step approach (or six or seven steps as often is the case).

First learn how to stand at the foul line and release the ball, having the ball come off the thumb first, then the fingers. The

one-step approach will help the bowlers develop the pendulum swing. They should keep the arm straight and the left knee bent for right-handed bowlers (arm straight and right knee bent for left-handers) and the bowling shoulder aligned with the target.

If they are too small to do anything but swing the ball at the foul line, they should at least learn about lane targets which can help them roll the ball toward the headpin.

Learning to hit the headpin is a good lesson for young bowlers who aren't ready to master many fundamentals. Try to discourage the young ones from running to the foul line, carrying the ball until they reach the line, then dropping it out on the lane. They see others do it, so they want to.

Being like everyone else can lead to bad habits which will be more difficult to correct when they are older and able to take an approach properly.

The weight of the bowling ball should correlate with the growth and strength of the bowler. While senior bowlers often must reduce the weight of the ball they use due to reduction in strength and stamina, young bowlers should increase the weight of the ball gradually. As the body grows stronger, the 10-pound ball becomes easier to roll down the lane. And the span becomes too short as the hand grows.

During the growing years, a youngster's ball should be replaced about every two years. Rather than buying a new ball, the old one can be plugged and re-drilled. That will take care of the right span, but it does not compensate for the need to increase weight. There are house balls and they can be adequate, particularly if you don't want to keep buying new balls for young bowlers. But if a bowler is serious about the game and shows improvement, buying a new ball every two years is not extreme if the expense leads to a lifetime of pleasure, bowling the right way. If you don't feel purchasing a bowling ball is best, ask the league instructor or house manager to help pick out a house ball. The importance of the proper fit can't be overemphasized.

What about the bowler who has been playing the game without instruction?

First, youth must be made to believe the right way to bowl is best. Often that's in direct conflict with the way bowlers think they should bowl. "I can do it better this way," is a common reply when a coach tries to teach the right way to bowl. It is very difficult to break habits, particularly if the bowler has been doing things the wrong way for several years. But the 10 or 12-year-old

understands, the right way to bowl will carry through and be retained during adult years.

Bowling becomes a habit, and so does how to roll the ball. If youth learn the correct way first, bad habits might occur later, but not usually in the fundamentals.

It can be difficult to convince anyone who is bowling higher scores than the rest of the group that the ball is not being rolled correctly. And chances are the scores will improve slightly as more strength and experience are added. But the young bowler who is not following the correct way to roll the ball probably never will be a high average player. The coach must convince the bowler by changing, the scoring could drop, but eventually will go well beyond the present scoring.

Walk slowly to the foul line. Rushing – making that mad dash to get extra speed on the ball – is wasted energy and can be put to better use.

HOW TO IMPROVE

Youth bowlers with ability who are ready to move up the scoring ladder most likely will hit a peak. Learning more about the game, playing lanes and making adjustments become necessary. Often a bowler in a particular age group gets to be the best of the group. Becoming content is harmful. That's the time to improve.

Often the bowler's score will go down when others in the group improve. That's when it's time to practice, work on the game and get help from a qualified coach! It's time to check the minute details, virtually impossible without qualified help. The bowler needs to checklist hand position, proper thumb position, good knee bend, swinging through the target, checking follow through, etc. Study the spare system (see page 51) and learn adjustments.

AT WHAT AGE SHOULD A CHILD BEGIN BOWLING?

There's no set age. Mostly, it depends on how big and strong a child is and when the bowler can handle the ball.

If the youth can't handle a four-step approach it doesn't mean there's no chance to learn how to bowl. The youth should stand at the foul line and learn the straight arm swing and understand the lane targets help guide them to hitting the headpin.

Learning the basics, such as knowing the headpin is the target, can be taught at any age. If the youngster is strong enough to handle the ball and the four-step approach, that's the starting point. And the more fundamentals are practiced, the easier they become. The right way to bowl becomes the easiest and most natural way.

Youth should always bowl with supervision. Working with a USA Junior Olympic Bowling coach is a great place to start. To find one in your area, contact USA Bowling at 414/421-9008.

If there is one lesson for new bowlers to learn it is to walk slowly toward the foul line. It cannot be stressed too much: **EXCESSIVE SPEED IS NOT THE ANSWER TO HIGH SCORING.** And ability is not dependent upon size.

Any bowler can be proficient. It's not speed or power, but practice and the ability to adapt your fundamentals to the lanes.

Good bowling takes time and practice. But bowling is fun and can lead to a lifetime of enjoyment regardless of the level of ability. Learn the basics early. Create good habits. They'll always pay off.

One of the unique things about bowling is it doesn't matter what your age is, how big you are or how fast you can run. Physical or mental challenges also pose no barrier to competing.

Bowling is lucky to have several groups meeting the needs of these special people. They make it possible for more people to enjoy the sport. While these groups are not officially part of the American Bowling Congress, Women's International Bowling Congress or Young American Bowling Alliance, they share a mutual bond and often work together on a variety of events.

AMERICAN BLIND BOWLING ASSOCIATION

The American Blind Bowling Association annually sanctions more than 2,000 bowlers from approximately 100 bowling leagues, ABBA sanctioned leagues are required to follow all ABC/ WIBC playing and league rules.

ABBA active members must be legally blind which is defined as vision no better than 20/200 even with glasses or a limited field of 20 degrees or less. Sighted bowlers may join ABBA as auxiliary members.

In most blind bowling leagues, one sighted person, who serves as scorekeeper and pincaller, bowls with each team. Blind bowlers use the aid of special guide rails to help them compete. Guide rails may be purchased at cost from ABBA.

The ABBA Annual Championship Tournament is held over the Memorial Day weekend. Bowlers compete for both scratch and handicap prizes in team, doubles and singles events. Area associations also conduct annual regional tournaments.

ABBA also publishes a newsletter "The Blind Bowler," three times a year in large print and Braille and on cassette tape. Anyone wanting to receive the publication, wishing more information about the organization or finding out how to join should write to: Judy Refosco, ABBA Secretary Treasurer, 315 Main St., Houston, PA 15342, phone (724) 745-5986.

AMERICAN WHEELCHAIR BOWLING ASSOCIATION

The American Wheelchair Bowling Association is a non-profit organization of wheelchair bowlers, dedicated to encouraging, developing and regulating wheelchair bowling and wheelchair bowling leagues.

Started in 1962 with 33 members, the AWBA today serves wheelchair bowlers in nearly every state and several foreign countries. The AWBA serves to strengthen existing wheelchair clubs and leagues and helps independent bowlers start new leagues. It strives to help all wheelchair bowlers with any problems they confront. It works in conjunction with ABC and WIBC on rules with special provisions for its members.

If you are disabled, confined to a wheelchair and interested in bowling, AWBA encourages you to become a member. As an AWBA member, you join wheelchair bowlers who compete under the same rules and regulations. The AWBA offers wheelchair bowlers official tournament competitions as well.

For more information about the AWBA, contact Executive Secretary/ Treasurer George Snyder, 6264 North Andrews Ave., Ft. Lauderdale, FL 33309, phone/FAX (954) 491-2886.

BOWLER'S TO VETERANS LINK

The Bowler's to Veterans Link is America's only national sports organization specifically devoted to supporting recreational and therapeutic programs for veterans.

Each year it provides hospitalized and those receiving outpatient services at Veterans Administration medical centers with programs and equipment to help speed recovery and boost their spirits. It accomplishes this through cash grants for recreational equipment, touring entertainment troupes, sponsorship of visiting celebrity bowlers and much more.

Since inception in 1942 as the Bowlers Victory Legion, BVL volunteers have raised more than $26 million to support the rehabilitation of veterans. It is supported by America's bowlers through fund raisers held by thousands of local bowling associations each year.

For more information, contact BVL at P.O. Box 2289, Rockville, MD 20847-2289, phone (301) 881-8333, fax (301) 881-4042.

NATIONAL DEAF BOWLING ASSOCIATION

The National Deaf Bowling Association was organized in 1964 by Neil Jones, a bowler from San Jose, Calif., who put together a tournament for deaf bowlers from throughout the United States. It later expanded to include deaf bowlers worldwide.

The group conducts an annual tournament at sites throughout the United States. It also sanctions events at the local, state and regional levels and works closely with regional deaf bowling associations.

For more information about the National Deaf Bowling Association, contact Roger Sellers, 950 Hwy 1 North, McGehee, AR 71654-9705, TDD (870) 222-5640, FAX (870) 222-5641.

SPECIAL OLYMPICS

Special Olympics, founded by Eunice Kennedy in 1968, is a world-wide program of sports training and competition for athletes with mental retardation. Supported by more than 500,000 volunteers, Special Olympics has chapters in all 50 states and more than 120 countries.

Special Olympics training and competition takes place year-round in both summer and winter events. Approximately 500,000 athletes participate in bowling, making it the second largest Special Olympics sport behind track and field.

ABC annually hosts a national Special Olympics Unified Tournament prior to the start of its annual championships. Unified Sports is a pioneer program that puts Special Olympics athletes and athletes with mental retardation together on the same team. As their averages improve, Special Olympians can be moved by their coaches to compete as non-Special Olympics partners.

Special Olympics volunteers are always needed. Contact your local Special Olympics chapter for more information.

With the camaraderie it promotes, and its accessibility to people of all ages, social classes, and physical abilities, bowling is the ideal pursuit for fund raising activities. Each year, more than $73 million are raised for numerous local and national charities and scholarship programs. Simply stated, bowling gives back to the community like no other recreational industry.

To that end, Bowling Gives has been created by the major bowling organizations. The goal

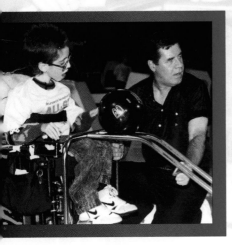

of Bowling Gives is to unify and further strengthen the industry's vast efforts in raising funds for a variety of worthy causes. Bowling Gives develops new partnerships with national cause related groups to expand the already vast potential of bowling as a driving force in grass roots fund raising.

How does Bowling Gives tackle such a challenging endeavor? Through an ongoing campaign, it sets annual goals for the bowling industry to raise millions of dollars through new and existing

cause-related efforts. The campaign incorporates a variety of elements, including:

• Creating new relationships with national cause related organizations, such as the Susan G. Komen Breast Cancer Foundation.

• An expanded relationship with the Muscular Dystrophy Association.

• Providing educational material to proprietors and local associations about fundraising.

• The use of high profile sports and entertainment figures for fund raising and public relations functions.

• National and grass roots public relations efforts.

With the continued support of the Bowling, Inc. partners, its many dedicated members and volunteers, bowling can raise the bar from $73 million annually to far greater heights. The old saying, "There's strength in numbers" rings so true for bowling, especially when Bowling Gives.

bowling gives

—| A |—

ABBA – American Blind Bowling Association, an organization of blind bowlers.

ABC – American Bowling Congress, world's largest sports membership organization, official rule-making body of tenpin bowling for its members in United States, Canada, Puerto Rico and military bases worldwide. Founded in 1895.

ACUI – Association of College Unions International which recognizes several sports, including bowling.

AMF – One of major developers and manufacturers in industry. Also owns and operates hundreds of centers worldwide. Name derives from founding American Machine & Foundry Inc.

AWBA – American Wheelchair Bowling Association, an organization of bowlers who compete from wheelchairs.

ACTION – When bowlers compete for money. See Pot Games.

ACTUAL (also SCRATCH) – Bowling without benefit of handicap or bonus.

ADJUST – When a bowler makes changes in his/her starting point on the approach and/or target on the lane during competition.

ALLEY (also LANE and BED) – Playing surface made of either maple and pine boards, or a synthetic surface.

ALLEY BALL (also HOUSE BALL) – Using a ball provided by the center.

ALL EVENTS – A combined total score of singles, doubles and team event.

ALL THE WAY (also PUNCH OUT, BACK ____, OFF THE SHEET) – Finishing a game from any frame with nothing but strikes.

AMBASSADORS – Professional bowlers who represent ABC at various functions.

ANCHOR – Last player in lineup for team competition.

ANDY VARIPAPA 300 – ABC Hall of Famer Andy Varipapa, in his countless exhibitions, called 12 strikes in a row, no matter where they started, a 300 game.

APPLE – Term used for bowling ball many years ago. Also to describe bowler who fails to come through in clutch situation. Sometimes also a description for a flat ball.

APPROACH (also RUNWAY) – Portion of lane behind foul line used by bowlers to build momentum to delivery.

ARROWS – Aiming points embedded in the lanes starting about 15 feet from the foul line.

ASSOCIATIONS – Name applied to volunteer organizations serving at the local, state and provincial levels for the betterment of the membership organizations.

BBIA – Billiard and Bowling Institute of America, an organization of firms and groups in both industries.

BPAA – Bowling Proprietors Association of America, an organization for proprietors from the United States and Canada, plus some other international locations.

BWAA – Bowling Writers Association of America, an organization of media representatives from throughout the world.

BABY THE BALL – Releasing the ball without authority, therefore failing to get maximum results.

BABY SPLIT – The 2-7, 3-10, 4-5, 5-6, 7-8, 8-9, 9-10 splits.

BACK _____ (can be any number) – See All The Way.

BACK UP (also REVERSE) – A ball a bowler throws which hooks towards the hand which he/she delivers it. Example, a right-hander who hooks the ball to the right.

BAKER SYSTEM – A format which calls for different bowlers executing in different frames. Mainly used in five-person team competition where the No. 1 bowler throws in the first and sixth frames, the No. 2 bowler in the second and seventh, etc.

BALK – An incomplete approach in which the bowler stops before delivering a ball. This may even be done beyond the foul line and the bowler is not penalized for a delivery.

BALL RACK – Where the ball rests in the settee area after its return following a delivery. Also used to describe where establishments keep house balls.

BALL TRACK – Area of lane where the majority of balls are rolled. Also the worn ring around a ball from continuous contact with the lane surface.

BALL WEIGHTS – A ball cannot exceed 16 pounds. Manufacturers put a massive weight in some portion of the ball (usually under the label) to allow ball drillers to place weights in different areas to gain various ball reaction. The maximum weight allowed is a 3 ounce variance between top and bottom and 1 ounce variance between the sides in balls weighing 10 pounds or more.

BED – See Alley.

BEDPOSTS (also BIG FOUR, DOUBLE PINOCHLE) – The 4-6-7-10 split.

BEER FRAME – Used in team competition to determine who buys liquid refreshments, either when all but one player strikes or in a designated frame (usually the fifth) for the bowler with the fewest pins on the first ball.

BELLY THE BALL – Increasing a ball's hook by releasing it in a sharp direction towards the channel and hooking it back into the pocket.

BENCH WORK – Jockeying, conversation or other actions intended to upset an opponent.

BIG BALL – Either a crucial shot in a match or a working hook that enables a bowler to carry strikes on something less than perfect pocket hits.

BIG FILL – Nine or 10 pins on any shot, usually more applicable to the final ball in the 10th frame.

BIG FOUR – See Bedposts.

BLIND – Score allowed for absent member, usually lower than his/her average as a penalty.

BLOCKED (also PIE, TRACKED, SLOTS) – A lane which is deliberately dressed to create an easy path to the pocket to increase scoring potential.

BLOW (also ERROR, MISS) – A missed spare.

BLOW THE RACK – Can be applied for a variety of strikes – a light sweeping strike, carrying all 10 pins into the pin or a solid hit.

BLOWOUT – Downing all the pins but one.

BOARD – Wooden lanes have approximately one-inch boards standing on end while synthetic lanes feature the same image. Bowlers pick specific boards as their target on various shots. The "fifth board" is the "first arrow," the 10th board the "second arrow," etc.

BOCCI STYLE – A bowler who finishes his/her approach on the wrong foot. This is style used in Italian game of the same name.

BODY ENGLISH – Contortion of the arms, legs and body in hopes of steering the ball after it has left the hand.

BONUS – Used in match play bowling for winning a particular match. It can be one, two or more games in a particular match and the bonus may be between 10 and 50 extra pins.

BOX (also CANTO) – Frame.

BREAK – When something very fortunate happens, such as late pinfall. Also used to indicate the end of a string of strikes.

BREAK POINT – Point on the lane where the ball begins to hook toward the pins.

BRIDGE – The span separating the finger holes on a bowling ball.

BROOKLYN (also CROSSOVER) – A strike when the ball goes to the opposite side it was intended to go. For example, a right-hander hitting the left side of the head pin. (In Brooklyn it is called a Jersey.)

BROOM BALL – A ball that hits the pocket in such a way that pins scatter as though they were swept with a broom.

BRUNSWICK – One of major developers and manufacturers in industry, and owner of more than 100 centers throughout the world.

BUCKET – The 2-4-5-8 or 3-5-6-9 spare leaves.

CC – Double century or 200 game.

CTF – Canadian Tenpin Federation, an organization which conducts competition and selects teams to represent its country in international competition.

CANTO – See Box and Frame.

CENTURY AWARD – An award presented to a bowler for exceeding his/her average by at least 100 pins.

CERTIFICATION – All recognized centers must have their lanes certified by ABC/ WIBC annually. Bowling is the only sport which has such a program to insure all of its "playing fields" are checked to meet certain specifications on a yearly basis.

CHANNEL
(also GUTTER) – That dreaded depression to the right and left of the lane, guiding the ball to the pit once it leaves the playing area.

CHARGE – When an individual or team begins its momentum to move towards the top of the standings.

CHEESECAKES – Easy scoring lanes.

CHERRY
(also CHOP, PICK) – Chopping the front pin of spare leave while a pin behind or alongside remains standing.

CHEVRON (also EMBLEM) – An award given for a bowling accomplishment which can be applied to a bowling shirt or in a display.

CHICKEN TRACKS – A string of strikes on the scoresheet.

CHOKE – Used to describe a bowler's performance when he/she fails to perform well in a clutch situation.

CLASSIFIED – Leagues or tournaments with average limitations or other restrictions.

CLEAN GAME – A game with spares or strikes in every frame.

CLOTHES LINE – The 1-2-4-7 or 1-3-6-10 spare leave.

CLUTCH – Coming through in a pressure situation.

CONVERT – Knock down the remaining pins on the lane for a spare.

COUNT – Number of pins knocked down on each first ball.

CORE (Also WEIGHT BLOCK) – The solid massive weight in a bowling ball, usually under the label. Used to provide balance (See Ball Weights) as to the wishes of the ball's owner.

CRANKER – A bowler who throws a wide hook, usually by snapping the wrist sharply at the release point.

CREEPER – A ball progressing down the lane very slowly.

CROOKED ARM – Having the elbow far from the body on the downswing and release.

CROSSOVER – See Brooklyn.

CURVE – The path of the ball from the release to pin contact.

CUSHION – The padding at the rear of the pit to absorb the shock of the ball and pins.

DEAD BALL (Also FLAT BALL, NOTHING BALL, PUMPKIN, ROLL OUT) – An ineffective ball which fades or deflects badly when it hits the pins. Also can be declared at delivery if any of a variety of factors occur as listed in the ABC Rule Book.

DEAD WOOD – Pins which fall over but remain on the lane or in the channel which must be removed before the next shot.

DEFLECTION – The movement of the ball after it hits the pins.

DELIVERY – The combination of a bowler's approach and release.

DEUCE – 200 game or average.

DIME STORE – The 5-10 split.

DITCH – Playing a severe outside line, sending the ball right next to the channel.

DIVE – The action of a big hook ball at the last second before it hits the pins.

DODO – A term used years ago for balls loaded with weights to make them overweight or have improper balance. Also refers to the scale used to measure the weights in a ball.

DOTS – Imbedded in the lane just over the foul line and used by some bowlers as their target.

DOUBLE – Two consecutive strikes.

DOUBLE PINOCHLE – See Bedposts.

DOUBLE TAP – Leaving the 7-10 split on a seemingly good pocket hit.

DOUBLE WOOD (also **SLEEPER, TANDEM**) – When one pin is directly behind the other, especially two pins such as the 1-5, 2-8 or 3-9.

DOUGHNUT – Same as a split.

DOVETAIL – Where the maple (dark) and pine (light) boards join.

DRESSING (Also **OIL**) – The substance used to coat or dress the lanes, a necessity to protect the lane surface. Usually has a mineral oil base.

DRIVE – An old term for an alley, it now is the revolving action of a ball as it comes in contact with the pins.

DRY LANE – A lane which has little dressing, causing the ball to hook drastically.

DUROMETER TEST – An instrument which inserts a needle into the ball's surface to determine its hardness. Minimum hardness specifications are: ABC, 72; PBA, 75.

DUTCH 200 – A 200 game scored by alternating strikes and spares.

EMBLEM – See Chevron.

ERROR – See Blow.

FIQ – Federation Internationale des Quilleurs, the organization responsible for worldwide amateur competition with more than 85 member nations.

FAITH, HOPE and CHARITY – The 2-7-10 or 3-7-10 splits.

FAST (also **RUNNING**) – Mainly refers to a lane hooking considerably, but in some areas it refers to the condition restricting the hook.

FAST EIGHT – A pocket hit that leaves the 4-7 or 6-10.

FENCE POSTS (Also **GOAL POSTS, SNAKE EYES**) – The 7-10 split.

FIELD GOAL – Rolling a ball between a split and not touching any.

FILL – Pins knocked down following a spare or two or more consecutive strikes.

FIT SPLIT – Any split where the ball can hit both pins.

FLAT BALL – See Dead Ball.

FOUL – Touching or going beyond the foul line with any body part at delivery.

FOUL JUDGE – Person who sits at foul line to make sure bowlers do not go over the foul line. Necessity prior to electronic foul detectors, but now only used when detectors are not working.

FOUL LINE – Solid stripe, usually black, which separates the approach from the lane.

FOUNDATION – A ninth frame strike. An early foundation is an eighth frame strike.

FRAME – Each game is divided into 10 frames, the first nine allowing a maximum of two shots with three shots allowed in the 10th frame.

FRONT FIVE, SIX, ETC. – The number of consecutive strikes at the start of a game.

FROZEN ROPE – A ball rolled with excessive speed almost straight into the pocket.

FULL HIT (also HIGH HIT) – A ball striking near the center of the head pin on a strike attempt, or the middle of any pin at which you are aiming.

FULL ROLLER – A ball that rolls over its full circumference and produces a track between the thumb and fingers.

GETTING THE WOOD – Making sure you take down as many pins as possible on a wide open split.

GOAL POSTS – See Fence Posts.

GRAB – The friction between the lane and ball results in a sudden hook.

GRAVEYARDS – Low scoring lanes.

GREEK CHURCH – The 4-6-7-8-10 or 4-6-7-9-10 leave.

GRABBING THE LANE – At some point down the lane, friction between the ball and the lane surface causes the ball speed to slow down, and the ball will "grab" the lane.

GROOVE – The ball track on the lane. Also applies to a bowler who is performing well and has his fundamentals mechanically perfect.

GUTTER – See Channel.

GUTTER BALL (Also POODLE) – A ball which falls into the channel before hitting the pins.

HALF HIT – Midway between a full and light hit, many times resulting in leaving a corner pin (7 or 10).

HANDICAP – Pins awarded to individuals or teams in an attempt to equalize the competition.

HARD WAY – Rolling a Dutch 200, or converting a spare in an unconventional manner.

HEADS – The first 16 feet of the lane beyond the foul line.

HEADPIN – The 1 pin.

HIGH BOARD – During the course of pounding by heavy bowling balls, a board on the lane may loosen and rise slightly. Atmospheric conditions also may cause a board to expand or contract slightly.

HIGH HIT – See Full Hit.

HITTING UP – Bowlers who release the ball late on the upswing.

HOLD – An area on the lane that resists hook action of the ball, preventing it from hooking high on the head pin.

HOLE (also POCKET) – Solidly between the 1-3 pins for right-handers and between the 1-2 for lefthanders.

HOME ALLEY – Favorite establishment for a team or individual, or the favorite pair of lanes in an establishment.

HOOK – A ball path that curves.

HOOKING LANE – A lane on which the ball hooks more than usual.

HOT – When a bowler or team starts stringing strikes.

HOUSE BALL – Bowling balls provided by the center.

IBM/HF – International Bowling Museum and Hall of Fame located in downtown St. Louis.

IBPSIA – International Bowling Pro Shop and Instructors Association, an organization of pro shop owners, instructors and manufacturers.

INSIDE – A line used by a bowler who plays toward the center of the lane, using the third, fourth or fifth arrows.

JERSEY – The reference to a crossover strike in some areas, especially in Brooklyn. Also a crossover strike by a lefthander.

KEGLER – German word for bowler, and since the sport was brought to this continent by Germans, the term used to describe bowlers for many years.

KICKBACK – Vertical division boards between lanes in the pit. On most hits, the pins bounce off the kickbacks to knock down additional pins.

KINGPIN – Varies in areas, sometimes the head pin (1) otherwise the 5.

KING OF THE HILL – A special match which pits the most recent champion of an event against a previous champion who earned the title in competition against other champions.

KITTY (also POT) – Money collected from team members for a variety of reasons – misses, low games, below average, etc. May also be tournament winnings. Used to defray expenses for tournaments or divided equally at season's end.

LABEL – The manufacturer's marking on the ball, pin or lane.

LANE – See Alley.

LATE 10 OR 7 – When the corner pin hesitates before falling on a strike.

LEADOFF – First player in team lineup.

LEVERAGE – Being in the proper release position at the foul line, usually with the knee solidly under the body, to allow maximum power in rolling the ball.

LIFT – Giving the ball upward motion with the fingers at the point of release to increase the amount a ball will hook.

LIGHT – Not full on the target pin, for righthanders too much to the right.

LILY (also SOUR APPLE) – The 5-7-10 split.

LINE – This has two meanings, the path a bowling ball takes from release to the pocket, and one game of bowling.

LOFTING – Throwing the ball well out on the lane, not rolling it.

LOOPER – Extra wide, usually slow, hook ball.

the lane the bowler is using as his/her target.

MATCH PLAY – Portion of tournament or league play where bowlers are pitted against each other.

MEDAL PLAY – Strictly total pinfall.

MESSENGER – A pin which rolls across the lane bed to knock down additional pins.

MILL HOLE – A small hole drilled in a ball to test its hardness.

MISS – See Blow.

MIXED LEAGUES – Organized leagues of men and women competing together, unless members of same organization.

MIXER – A ball with action that causes the pins to bounce around.

MOVE IN – Adjusting your starting and/or target point, for right-handers further to the left.

MOVE OUT – Adjusting your starting and/or target point, for right-handers further to the right.

MULE EARS – The 7-10 split.

MUBIG – Multi-Unit Bowling Information Group composed of individuals who own several centers.

MAPLE – A very hard wood used in lane approaches, headers, pin decks and pins.

MAPLES – Reference sometimes made to pins, especially when pins were made of solid maple.

MARK – This has two meanings, a strike or spare, or the spot on

NAIR – National Association of Independent Resurfacers, composed of firms which resurface lanes on a regular basis to ensure they comply with specifications.

NDBA – The National Deaf Bowling Association, an organization of deaf bowlers.

NWBA – National Women Bowling Writers, an organization

of mainly women bowling writers in the U.S. and Canada.

NATIONAL BOWLING STADIUM – A state-of-the-art bowling arena in Reno, Nev., open in 1995.

NO TAP – A form of competition when strikes are awarded for nine pin hits, and some time for eight pins, as well as strikes.

NOSE HIT – When the ball hits flush on the head pin.

NOTHING BALL – See Dead Ball.

OFF THE SHEET – See All The Way.

OIL – See Dressing.

OILY (Also SLICK and STIFF) – Indicates there is a heavy coating of dressing on the lanes, making it difficult to hook a ball.

OPEN – A frame that doesn't produce a strike or spare.

OPEN BOWLING – Non-league or non-tournament play, for fun or practice.

OUT AND IN – Throwing a wide hook, for a right-hander starting from the far left of the approach and sending the ball towards the right gutter.

OUTSIDE – A way to play the lanes from the corner, for example throwing over the first arrow.

OVER – In tournament play 200 is used as par and if an individual is averaging above that figure, he/she is that total number of pins over.

OVER TURN – To apply too much spin to the ball and not enough finger lift.

PBA – Professional Bowlers Association, the organization that governs the professional tour for men.

PACK – Roll a flush, solid strike.

PART OF THE BUILDING (Also SOLID, RAP, TAP) – A single pin that stands after a seemingly perfect shot.

PERFECT GAME – Rolling 12 consecutive strikes in one game for 300.

PLASTIC BALLS – Developed during the 1950s and made of polyester.

PIE ALLEY – See Blocked.

PIN – A pin must weigh between 3 pounds, 6 ounces and 3 pounds, 10 ounces. It is 15 inches high and 15 inches in circumference at its broadest point.

PIN DECK – The area where the pins are set.

PINCHING THE BALL – Gripping the ball too tightly.

PINE – Softer wood used beyond division boards, usually lighter wood, in the mid-portion of the lane.

PIT – Open area behind pin deck where pins and balls gather.

PITCH – Angle at which holes in bowling ball are drilled.

POCKET – See Hole.

POCKET SPLIT (Also STRIKE SPLIT) – A split left after a seemingly perfect shot.

POINT -- To send the ball more directly towards the pocket.

POODLE – See Gutter Ball.

POSITION ROUNDS – Part of leagues or tournaments when teams or players face each other based on their standings. Example, first place meets second, third meets fourth, etc.

POT GAME – Competition in which two or more bowlers post some sort of stake to be divided depending upon number of entries, or on a winner take all basis.

PUNCH OUT – See Off The Sheet, but usually refers to striking out in 10th frame.

PUMPKIN – See Dead Ball. Also term for bowling ball in some areas.

PWBA – Professional Women's Bowling Association, the organization which governs the professional tour for women.

RAILROAD – An old term used for splits.

RAP – See Part Of The Building.

REACTIVE RESIN BALLS – Developed in the 1990s, made of an advanced urethane.

READING THE LANES – Discovering whether a lane hooks or holds, and where the best place to roll the ball to score high.

REGIONAL PLAYER – Part of the PBA structure is regional competition for members who participate in weekend events.

RELEASE POINT – The exact point where a bowler releases the ball at the foul line.

RESURFACE – When a center removes the lane finish to bare wood in preparation for recoating the lane finish.

RETURN – The track on which balls roll from the pit to ball rack.

REVERSE – See Backup.

REVOLUTIONS – Also known as revs. The number of turns a ball takes to go from the foul line to the pins.

ROLL OUT – See Dead Ball.

RUNWAY – See Approach.

RUN IT OUT – When a bowler moves swiftly parallel to the foul line after his/her release to root home a strike.

RUNNING LANE – See Fast.

SANCTIONED – Bowling competition conducted in accordance with ABC, WIBC or YABA rules, on equipment manufactured and installed to the organizations' specifications and, in the case of tournaments, handling and disbursing prize fund in accordance with the prize formula mandated by the organizations.

SANDBAGGER – Bowler who purposely keeps his/her average down in order to receive a higher handicap.

SCENIC ROUTE – Path taken by a big hook ball.

SCOTCH DOUBLES – Where partners alternate shots.

SCRATCH – See Actual.

SENIOR – ABC and WIBC have special awards and handicap events for members 55 and over, including their organization's Senior Championships. PBA has a special classification for members 50 years and older which has its own Tour.

SET – Ball holding into the pocket.

SETTEE – The bowlers area between the approach and concourse.

SHOTGUN SHOT – Rolling the ball from the hip, meaning the bowler does not bend his/her knees far enough.

SHORT PIN – A rolling or spinning pin on the pin deck which just fails to knock down a standing pin.

SIDEARMING – Allowing the entire arm to swing away from the body during the swing arc.

SKID – Because of the speed of the ball when it is released, it "skids" in the first portion of the lane before the finger lift imparted at the release starts it into a sideways spin.

SLEEPER – See Double Wood.

SLICK – See Oily.

SLOTS – See Blocked.

SNAKE EYES – See Fence Posts.

SNOW PLOW – A ball that hits straight on the head pin and clears the pins for a strike.

SOLDIER – A hidden pin, such as the 8 behind the 2.

SOLID – See Part Of The Building.

SOUR APPLE – See Lily.

SPAN – The distance between the thumb and finger holes on a bowling ball.

SPARE – Knocking down all 10 pins with two balls.

SPARE LEAVE – Pins standing after first ball.

SPILLER – A light strike in which the pins seem to fall slowly, taking a longer time than usual.

SPLIT – A spare leave in which the head pin is down and the remaining combination of pins have a gap in them, ranging from the 4-5 to the 7-10.

SPOT – A target on lane at which the bowler aims, ranging from a dot, to an arrow, to a dark board.

STEAL – Get more pins than you deserve on a questionable hit.

STEPLADDER – Finals made popular by television where a specified number of entrants qualify for a match play competition.

STIFF – See Oily.

STONE 10 – Leaving a 10 pin on a seemingly solid first ball.

STRAP THE BALL – Applying maximum lift on a shot.

STRIKE – Knocking down all 10 pins on the first ball.

STRIKE OUT – See Off The Sheet.

STRIKE SPLIT – See Pocket Split.

STRIKE TEN ENTERTAINMENT – Marketing company for many of the major bowling organizations.

STRING – A number of continuous strikes.

STROKER – Bowlers who get to the line smoothly, have a good release and roll the ball with much less hook.

SURLYN – The cover material for most bowling pins.

SWEEPER – A form of pot game competition that usually is conducted in association with another tournament.

SWEEPSTAKE – A term for a bowling tournament at one time.

SWING ARC – The plane the arm takes from the time it starts to when it ends.

SYNTHETIC LANES – A non-wood or manmade covering that may be placed over an existing wood lane, or a pre-constructed unit placed on a foundation. First installation was in late 1970s. Technological advancements have made them popular, coupled with the shortage and high cost of wooden lane replacements.

SYNTHETIC PINS – A non-wood or man made pin. A magnesium has been approved by ABC since 1962, but is not used in very many centers.

SYSTEM OF BOWLING – The set of uniform rules and standards for all major elements of the game (lane surface, balls, pins and lane dressing).

TNBA – The National Bowling Association, mainly a tournament organization formed many years ago when non-whites were not able to compete in regular competition.

TANDEM – See Double Wood.

TAP – See Rap.

TARGETING – Selecting a target on the lane for your ball to hit. Some use the dots, some the arrows, some a particular board and others particular pins.

TEAM USA – A team composed of men and women representing the United States in international competition.

TELEPHONE POLES – Heavy pins, also called trees.

THIN HIT – When the first ball barely touches the head pin.

TOPPING THE BALL – When fingers are on top of the ball instead of behind or to the side at ball release. Causes an ineffective ball with little action.

TRACKED – See Blocked. Also an old ball which is worn due to age.

TRIP 4 OR TRIP 6 – When the 4 or 6 pin is felled by another pin by a right-hander or lefthander, respectively, on the first ball.

TURKEY – Three consecutive strikes.

TURN – The hand motion which imparts rotation to a ball at release.

TWEENER – Between a cranker and a stroker in releasing the ball.

USA BOWLING – Recognized by the U.S. Olympic Committee as the organization responsible for amateur competition in the United States.

UNDER – In tournament play 200 is used for par and if an individual is averaging below that figure, he/she is that total number of pins under.

UP THE HILL – Coaxing a ball to go towards the pocket.

URETHENE – One of the biggest bowling ball manufacturing breakthroughs of bowling ball cover materials. Started in the 1980s and advanced over the years with technology.

URETHENE SPLIT – The 2-8-10 and 3-7-9 caused by the sharp breaking point of reactive resin balls.

either knocked down or received in handicapping.

WORLD TEAM CHALLENGE – A tournament originated by ABC designed to bring team bowling back into the forefront.

YABA – Young American Bowling Alliance, the organization governing competition from youths to collegians.

VENTING – Drilling a very small hole adjacent to the thumb hole of a ball to relieve suction.

VOID – An open area in a pin's center to control weight and center of gravity.

WBW – World Bowling Writers, composed of journalists throughout the world.

WIBC – Women's International Bowling Congress, the sister organization of ABC. Founded in 1916.

WASHOUT – To leave the 1-2-4-7-10, 1-2-4-10 or 1-2-10; or, 1-3-6-7-10, 1-3-6-7 or 1-3-7 after the first ball.

WATER IN THE BALL – A weak ball that deflects, sometimes creating crazy spare leaves.

WEIGHT BLOCK – See Core.

WOOD – The number of pins

American Blind Bowling Association
315 N. Main Street
Houston, PA 15342
(724) 745-5986

American Bowling Congress
5301 S. 76th Street
Greendale, WI 53129-1127
(414) 421-6400
(414) 421-1194 (FAX)
www.bowl.com

American Wheelchair Bowling Association
6264 N. Andrews Ave.
Ft. Lauderdale, FL 33309
(954) 491-2886 (phone/FAX)

Bowling Proprietors Association of America
615 Six Flags Dr.
Arlington, TX 76011
(817) 649-5105
(817) 633-2940 (FAX)
www.bowl.com

Bowling Writers Association of America
675 N. Brookfield Rd.
Brookfield, WI 53045
(414) 641-2003
(414) 641-2005
www.geocities.com/colosseum/stands/5958

Bowlers to Veterans Link Fund
P.O. Box 2289
Rockville, MD 20847-2289
(301) 881-8333
(301) 881-4042 (FAX)
www.his.com/~bvlfund

Federation Internationale des Quilleurs
1631 Mesa Avenue, Suite A
Colorado Springs, CO 80906
(719) 636-2695
(719) 636-3300 (FAX)
www.fiq.org

International Bowling Museum & Hall of Fame
111 Stadium Plaza
St. Louis, MO 63102
(314) 231-6340
(314) 231-4054 (FAX)
www.bowlingmuseum.com

International Bowling Pro Shop
and Instructors Association
P.O. Box 5634
Fresno, CA 93755
(800) 659-9444
(209) 275-9250 (FAX)
www.bowl.com

National Deaf
Bowling Association
950 Hwy 1 North
McGehee, AR 71654-9705
(870) 222-5640 (TDD)
(870) 222-5641 (FAX)

National Women Bowling Writers
3001 21st Street
Lubbock, TX 79410
(806) 795-3830 (phone/FAX)

Professional Bowlers Association
1720 Merriman Road
Akron, OH 44313
(330) 836-5568
(330) 836-2107 (FAX)
www.pbatour.com

Professional Women's Bowlers Association
7171 Cherryvale Boulevard
Rockford, IL 61112
(815) 332-5756
(815) 332-9636 (FAX)
www.pwba.com

The National Bowling Association
377 Park Avenue South, 7th Floor
New York, NY 10016
(212) 689-8308
(212) 725-5063 (FAX)
www.inlink.com/~tnbainc

USA Bowling
5301 S. 76th Street
Greendale, WI 53129
(414) 421-9008
(414) 421-9188 (FAX)
www.bowl.com

Women's International Bowling Congress
5301 South 76th Street
Greendale, WI 53129
(414) 421-9000
(414) 421-4420 (FAX)
www.bowl.com

Young American Bowling Alliance
5301 South 76th Street
Greendale, WI 53129
(414)421-4700
(414) 421-1301 (FAX)
www.bowl.com

If You're Really Good, We'll Hang You.

(In the Hall, that is.)

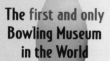

The first and only Bowling Museum in the World

Two Halls of Fame – the International Bowling and the St. Louis Cardinals

Three floors of great hands-on exhibits, depicting the history of the great game worldwide

Four frames of bowling FREE with your admission

Five thousand years of bowling history!

Two Sports Museums under One Roof!

Discover 5000 years of bowling history, from ancient Egypt to modern tenpins. Relive great moments in St. Louis Baseball History... three levels of fascination and fun... all for one admission!

Located across the street from Busch Stadium at Walnut and 7th Street in downtown St. Louis

International Bowling Museum and Hall of Fame
The Cardinals Hall of Fame
111 Stadium Plaza Drive, St. Louis, MO 63102
(314) 231-6340
www.bowlingmuseum.com